Faith is Not Blind

Crossing the Visible Bridge to the Invisible God

Jeffrey Kliewer

Scripture taken from the NEW AMERICAN STANDARD BIBLE®,
Copyright © 1960, 1962, 1963, 1968, 1971, 1972, 1973, 1975, 1977, 1995 by the Lockman Foundation. Used by permission.

Image Copyright Sergii Votit, Used under license from Shutterstock.com

Editing by Jeanette Windle, JM Windle Manuscript Services

Copyright © 2020 Faith House Publishers

All rights reserved.

ISBN: 978-0692217481
ISBN-13: 0692217487

DEDICATION

To my wonderful wife, who is the love of my life and my closest friend. Also to my parents, who taught me the Scriptures when I was young. And finally to my children, upon whom I desire to bestow the same invaluable blessing.

CONTENTS

ACKNOWLEDGEMENTS

I am very grateful to Bill Luebkemann, Pastor of Calvary Chapel of Marlton, NJ. His constant support opened the door of opportunity for me to write this book. I am also indebted to Fran Pultro, Pastor of Calvary Chapel on the King's Highway, Philadelphia PA, and my Professors at Dallas Theological Seminary for their excellent teaching, which contributed greatly to the content of the book.

INTRODUCTION

Believing in Jesus Christ does not require a blind leap of faith. It is not like stepping off a cliff into an abyss with the desperate hope that an invisible bridge will keep you from falling. Rather, the bridge is visible. It is there to be examined. You can see others crossing it ahead of you. You can even press your foot upon it to test it before stepping out. It may be scary, but eventually faith will require you to set your feet upon the planks. As you begin to cross over, with each progressive step, you will realize that the bridge does hold weight.

The bridge also holds promise. On the other side, there is peace for the troubled soul. There is rest for the overwhelmed. There is love for the jaded. There is healing for the wounded. There is joy for the downcast. There is friendship for the embattled. There is forgiveness for the sinner. There is real life available for the here and now, and there is eternal life that continues even after the grave.

Is this the place you've been searching for? Do you want to know if there really is a visible bridge that can get you there? If God Himself is cloaked from our sight, then is there anything to which we can look that might bring us to where He is?

Some say, "seeing is believing", but that doesn't account for every kind of seeing that there is. We all believe in gravity, magnetism, and the wind, but none of us have seen them, only their effects. We are only scared of stepping off a cliff because something has completely convinced us that gravity is real. We have seen the effect of gravity. We "see" magnetism when magnets hold papers to the refrigerator. We may only see the leaves, but we are just as certain about the reality of the wind that moves them. We can see that certain things are true even without seeing the thing itself.

When it comes to faith in God, *believing is seeing*—not with physical eyes, but with the eyes of the heart. Seeing God is an assurance, a certainty, a conviction in the heart. We can be just as convinced of the reality and goodness of God as we are convinced of the reality of our own hand that we hold out in front of our face. God dwells in a holy place, invisible to our physical eyes, but as surely as wind moves the leaf, God moves heaven and earth to reveal Himself to us. The invisible God has given us the visible bridge that we need. Without it, we couldn't step out in faith. Would you be willing to examine the bridge—even to step out upon it, little by little—if you knew where it is? What if there is some visible, audible, and tangible thing that is able to bring us to God?

Faith comes by hearing and hearing by the word of God (Romans 10:17).

God is not visible. His speech will not be audible. His skin cannot be touched. But the Word of God is the bridge we have been looking for. You can find God's Word on the pages of a Book printed with visible ink. You can read it yourself as you hold a Bible in your hands. You can hear someone read it verbatim or hear someone preach the substance of it. You can read a book like this that presents some of its main ideas. However it comes to you, God's Word has been passed down from generation to generation for thousands of years, a never-failing bridge that brings people to God.

There are 39 books written more than 400 years before the birth of Jesus that inspire faith in Him. Although Jesus Himself had not yet been seen, the writings were there to see and read. These words are still here with us! After Jesus came in the flesh, 27 more books were added to seal up the words of the prophets that went before. The 66 books of the Bible are the planks of the bridge that I ask you to walk upon. Specifically, I want to show you how the prophets revealed Jesus Christ long before He arrived, and in so doing, they proved that He was sent from heaven. Only God could have known such things about the future. The Old Testament foretells the most important Person and events in the history of the world. As we walk through the first 39 books, we will glance ahead at the additional 27 to see some of the ways those Old Testament promises found fulfillment.

The Word of God will be the bridge that takes us to the foot of the cross where Jesus died. He waits for you there. His arms are outstretched to welcome you, as He calls you to repent and believe. As you reach the last plank, you will see that Jesus stands there as the door to eternal life. When you step into Him by repenting and believing, your sins will be forgiven, you will be free, and you will be given eternal life.

I have been to the other side. Not the other side of physical death, but the starting point of eternal life. I can testify that the promise was fulfilled for me. When I put my faith in Jesus Christ, He gave me everything He promised and far more than anything this world has to offer. But He didn't immediately bring me into heaven. He left me here for a time with an assignment—to help others cross the bridge as well.

I am offering to walk with you as you cross the bridge to where God is. As we go, I will try to reassure you that the Word of God will hold up under your weight. But you have to learn to trust Him. That is what faith is—taking God at His Word, standing upon His promises. There are a thousand things that clamor for your attention, but the journey of faith is worth your time. You can take it step by step, one plank at a time. Perhaps you could read one chapter of this book a day for 39 days. I would expect that on the 40th day, as you read the conclusion, you would have faith to step into the embrace of Jesus Christ.

What specifically does that mean? Christianity is a faith that is built upon a message. We call that message "the Gospel", which simply means "the good news". The message pertains to a Person—Jesus Christ—and has seven elements to it, all of which are essential.

First, Jesus is the Son of God. He is actually equal with God the Father and the Spirit. Yet at the same time, Jesus is also fully human.

Second, He is the promised King who will one day bring His Kingdom.

Third, He died on a cross. The Gospel proposes that historically speaking, this literally happened.

Fourth, He died for the purpose of atoning for the sins of believers. He died as an innocent substitute in the place of guilty sinners.

Fifth, He literally and historically rose from the dead. His body—not just His spirit—resurrected.

Sixth, He now offers forgiveness of sin and eternal life as a free gift.

Seventh and finally, all one needs to do is trust Him for that free gift. Believing in Jesus to take sin away involves turning away from sin in order to turn to Him. That's called repentance. But it does not involve any good works or religious observances to add anything to what Jesus did. Salvation comes through faith alone. You need only to believe in this Jesus as revealed in the Gospel. Repent and call upon Him to save you, asking Him to come into your life. This is the seven-fold proposition—the extremely good news—that we bring.

I call you then to believe in the Lord Jesus Christ and be saved. I want to spend eternity with you in heaven. I am writing to those who were raised by Christians but are presently struggling as to whether or not they will own the faith of their parents. I am writing equally to those who were not raised to be Christian but who wonder if maybe there is evidence for this faith they observe in others. I am writing for the atheist, the agnostic, and the honest skeptic. I am writing to who I was twenty-plus years ago, a college student losing my religion and wondering if the bridge could really carry my weight.

Persuasive professors had shaken my faith in the reliability of the Bible. But sitting alone with my Bible in the middle of the night, I let it fall open to a random book of the Old Testament. That night, the Lord took me to Micah. Reading the fifth chapter, my faith in the Bible and in the Lord it reveals was resuscitated. At the time, I thought I had found in that random Scripture reading the needle in a haystack that was just what I needed. Now I know the miracle was not that I happened upon a certain book of the Bible. The miracle was far more profound than that and not really about me. The miracle was older than the coming of Jesus Christ Himself and was really about every one of us. The miracle is that no matter which of the 39 books of the Old Testament I might have flipped open to that night, it had within it supernatural evidence that Jesus is in fact—not just in faith—the Lord and Savior.

There are 39 books that provide ample reason to believe in Jesus Christ. What if I told you that Jesus is the God, Man, King, Priest, Sacrifice, Yahweh, Savior, Passover Lamb, Blood Atonement, Raised Serpent, Prophet, Captain, Deliverer, Redeemer, Rejected King, Davidic King, King of Peace, Miracle Worker, Ark of Salvation, Slow Judge, Fast Friend, Strong Defender, Great Reversal, Forsaken, Crucified, Word, Meaning of Life, Loving Husband, Virgin-born Son, Suffering Servant, New Covenant Maker, Weeping Prophet, Glory of the Lord, Messiah the Prince, Faithful Husband, Baptizer, Defender of the Weak, Betrayed by a Brother, Resurrected, Bethlehem Born, Wrath Satisfaction, Our Righteousness, Divider, Foundation, Humble, Prophesied Christ?

What if I told you that all of those things were said about Him more than 400 years before He was born to the Virgin Mary? If it proved true, then it would be a bridge to faith in the invisible God. The 39 chapters of this book correspond to the 39 books of the Old Testament. My goal in each chapter is to draw out from the text (not read into the text) the places where Jesus Christ is being revealed. In some of the longer books, the places were too many. For example, the first chapter is hardly a comprehensive listing of Christ's revelation in the book of Genesis. But I have included 5 major revelations because I intend to demonstrate that from the first book of the Old Testament alone, all the claims of the Christian Gospel are adequately supported. If we had nothing but Genesis, our faith would not be blind. Furthermore, the most essential aspects of Christ's person are revealed in the beginning. Genesis confirms His Deity, His humanity, His Kingdom, His Priesthood, and His Sacrifice. What a start we have in Genesis.

Since we have been taught for so long that faith is blind, I can imagine that there are objections to this notion that faith is based on something so solid. The first is likely to be the possibility of coincidence. Maybe by accident, Jesus just happened to fulfill what others had written. Dr. Peter Stoner, author of Science Speaks, calculated the probability of fulfilling 8 of the prophecies about the coming Messiah. For example, he calculated the odds of Jesus being born in Bethlehem to be 1 in 280,000. The odds of being betrayed by Judas were 1 in 1000. Entering Jerusalem riding on a donkey was 1 in a 100. Being crucified was 1 in 10,000. Yet each of these events was prophesied of the coming Messiah! The mathematical odds of one man fulfilling the 8 prophecies taken together were 1 in 10 to the 28th

power. That would be like covering the State of Texas in quarters piled three feet high, marking one with an X, and happening to grab the marked quarter on the first try while wearing a blindfold. Considering Dr. Stoner's statistical analysis, perhaps faith in Jesus is not so blind.

But someone else will object that the prophecies about Jesus do not prove what we say they do since there have been other successful prophets who are not in the Bible. Could the repetition of the predictive phenomenon render the Biblical record less impressive and inconclusive? For example, there is the most famous alleged extra-biblical future-telling prophet—Nostradamus. But this objection misses two crucial points. First, the Biblical prophets spoke clearly and contextually. They wrote simple narratives. The flow of thought is not convoluted. It is easy to follow. Linguists can trace the author's meaning precisely. Even an average Joe like me can read and follow the train of thought. So-called prophets like Nostradamus wrote strange and illogical prose.

Second, the promise of Messiah began in Genesis 3:15 and as future prophets spoke, they piled up information about one specific Person. With every prophecy, the field of potential candidates narrowed. For example, when Micah marked Bethlehem as the birthplace of Messiah, everyone who was born anywhere else in the world was eliminated. Nostradamus' prophecies continue to open up to more and more referents as history unfurls and more and more random events occur. For example, it was only a matter of time for an event like 9-11 to happen somewhere in the world and look similar to something that Nostradamus "prophesied".

So, whereas Nostradamus majors on vague language and a wide-open field of interpretation, Biblical prophets major on clear language and an ever-narrowing field of interpretation. That is why no such statistical probability as was deduced by Dr. Stoner could ever be applied to Nostradamus' writings. The bare truth is that there are no "prophetic" writings that can hold a candle to the Bible.

Another objection—that of collusion—is likewise difficult to maintain. Did the authors conspire to create the illusion of the supernatural fulfillment of predicted events? The authors of the 39 books lived in different places and were separated from each other by more than 1000 years. The unity of their subject matter is most remarkable considering the diversity of their times and cultures. For example, revelations came to Moses in Arabia around 1500 BC, to David in Judea around 1000 BC, and to Daniel in Persia around 500 BC. That we have so many independent witnesses is a great proof of the validity of their claim.

But perhaps these 39 books didn't actually have these prophecies. Maybe the New Testament authors doctored the documents and added things that would look like Jesus? This idea is a nonstarter since the Hebrew Scriptures (the 39 books of the Old Testament) were translated into various languages and disseminated for hundreds of years before the time of Christ. The Septuagint and the Targums are concrete examples. But if that were not enough, the Dead Sea Scrolls were discovered in 1947, and many of the actual extant manuscripts that were found predate the time of Jesus of

Nazareth. There probably isn't a textual scholar in the world who would argue that the prophecies addressed in this book were written after the fact. The position is untenable.

None of the objections are able to hold weight, but the words of the prophets do. No other religious claim or claim of any kind has a verifiably supernatural attestation. But the Gospel has 39 books that each prophesy about the coming Christ. Faith does not require them, but they do provide 39 sets of reasons to believe. They satisfy the human mind. God not only gave us the best news the world has ever heard, the message has an "according to". The Gospel is "according to" the Scriptures that preceded Christ. We're not judges called upon to weigh all this forthcoming evidence. We're guilty sinners who are mercifully given reasons to believe the Gospel by a God who uses these revelations to save some.

Much press is given to supposed contradictions or impossibilities in the Bible. There are answers to all these objections. Most are easy. Some are beyond me, but I am OK with that. I remember that "the secret things belong to the Lord our God, but the things which are revealed belong to us and our children forever" (Deuteronomy 29:29). But how little press is given to that which confirms the validity of the Bible and the Person of Jesus Christ. Many today do not understand the magnitude of the prophetic record. But the Gospel has always been based upon it.

The following 39 chapters offer a basis for faith in Jesus Christ. A visible bridge to faith in Jesus Christ will be illuminated. I hope you will find the time and the courage to step out upon it.

CHAPTER 1

SEEN IN THE BEGINNING
GENESIS

The first book of the Bible, Genesis—meaning "beginnings"—right away reveals God as the eternally existent uncaused Cause. Genesis opens with this most basic assertion, "in the beginning, God . . ." Fifty chapters unfold from there. They are filled with stories that are at least vaguely familiar to most adults. The serpent deceives Adam and Eve. Cain kills his own brother Abel. Noah and his family survive a worldwide flood. Abraham becomes the father of faith. Joseph's brothers sell him into slavery, but he rises as a ruler of Egypt.

Even those who have never read the stories have probably seen movies or otherwise become familiar enough with the stories to recognize references to them. But far fewer people understand that when God gave us the story of beginnings, He also hinted at the future. Moses wrote the Book of Genesis 1500 years before Jesus came. Yet Genesis gives us several distinct marks to identify God's

Son—Jesus Christ. There are at least five profound revelations of the Son of God, concerning Him being God, Man, King, Priest, and Sacrifice.

God

Genesis begins with "God", but the Hebrew title in Genesis 1:1 is an interesting revelation of what He is like. The word "Elohim" is actually a plural form. As the creation account unfolds and the entire Hebrew Bible from there, the repeated use of this title "Elohim" becomes more and more striking. After all, Judaism is strictly monotheistic. The Scriptures are replete with affirmations like the one found in Deuteronomy 6:4, "Hear, O Israel! The Lord is our God, the Lord is one!" And yet this plural title appears in the first verse of Genesis and will be used about 2500 times in the 39 books of the Hebrew Bible. Why would God be addressed as a plurality when He is only one God? The reader's curiosity continues to rise in that first chapter when "Elohim" creates humanity.

Let us make man in our image, according to our likeness (Genesis 1:26).

Since God alone is creating out of nothing, to whom is God speaking? Surely God is not speaking to angels since the Bible never presents them as Creators. But who else is there? Could it be that God is talking to Himself? As strange as it sounds to us, it would have been no less alarming to the original recipients of Genesis. Were the Book of Genesis ultimately of human origin, Moses surely would have written differently. Were the transmission process throughout the generations ultimately a human endeavor, if such an oddity had been written in the first place, then it certainly would have been edited through thousands of years of transmission. And yet it comes to us this way. God is strictly presented as one God, yet His most frequently used title is in the plural—"Elohim". God alone creates humanity in His own image, yet He addresses Himself with the pronouns "us" and "our".

The first verse ("Elohim") and the first chapter ("us" and "our") provide us with the first evidence that Jesus is God. When Jesus appears on the scene, He begins to identify Himself as being one with the Father (John 10:30). He claims to be God! Yet He repeatedly prays to His Father, carrying on conversation, the way distinct persons speak one with another. What's more, He tells us about a third person—the Holy Spirit—He intends to send to us after He returns to His Father (John 14). According to the claims of Jesus, the One *God* exists in Three *Persons.* From a human perspective, what got Jesus killed was the charge of blasphemy, which was based upon what Jesus said about his unique oneness with the Father and the Holy Spirit. Outraged, the religious leaders said, "You make yourself equal with God!" (John 10:33) But the first chapter of Genesis should have given them pause. It is reason enough for us to at least entertain the possibility that Jesus is God. Was He the One with whom the Father conversed in the beginning?

1500 years before Jesus came, as Moses wandered with the Israelites in the desert outside of Egypt, God inspired Moses to write an account of creation. In that first book of the Bible, Genesis, God called Himself "Elohim" (1:1). He revealed a conversation that took place between Father, Son, and Holy Spirit. "Let us make man in our image, according to our likeness" (1:26). It was a mark placed there for our good. The first sentence and the first chapter of the first book God gave to humankind reveals that there is only One *God* who eternally exists as more than one *Person.* This assertion was enigmatic for centuries, and in a sense it remains beyond our comprehension, but we have the claims of Jesus. God is one in essence, but there are three distinct Persons coexisting in the unity of His being. "Trinity" means "tri-unity" or "three in one". Jesus made claims to Deity that we are free to either accept or reject. But Genesis 1:1 and 1:26, by indicating plurality within God's unity, are the first evidence that makes those claims believable.

Man

There are two doctrines in Christian theology that trouble people perhaps more than any others. The first is this aforementioned idea of a "three-in-one" God. Christians alone think of God as Trinity. The second troubling proposition that we make is that Jesus is one Person with two natures. Jesus is 100% God *and* 100% human. Christians alone think of Jesus this way. We recognize that if we attempt to take anything away from either His Deity or His humanity, then we do violence to Him, because He is both. Yet we acknowledge that the idea of unfettered Deity forever taking on the constraints of human flesh is mind-blowing! Such a notion is in fact beyond where our human reasoning or our observations of the natural world would ever lead us. Belief in a Creator-God is revealed to all by the things that have been made. Belief in a God-Man requires special revelation. Even as the full Deity of Jesus Christ began to be revealed early in Genesis, so did His full humanity.

After Adam and Eve fall into sin, having eaten fruit from the one tree that was forbidden to them, they immediately begin the blame game. God looks to hold Adam responsible, but he points the finger at Eve. Eve, in turn, blames the Serpent that brought the temptation to her. In response, God will work His way up the chain, pronouncing judgment on every guilty party. But He begins with the Serpent.

It is important to realize, and the rest of the Bible will make this obvious, that the Serpent is more than a garden-variety snake. Behind the reptile is an intensely powerful and completely evil being named Lucifer (Satan or the Devil). Lucifer is a fallen angel. Having been expelled from heaven on account of his arrogant attempt to overthrow God's throne, he has become God's archenemy. Since God is all-powerful, He could destroy Satan. But evidently desiring to give His human creatures free will, He allowed Satan to tempt Adam and Eve.

This does not make God the author of evil, but rather of freedom. True worship becomes possible because people are able to respond to God's love. But sin and its consequences are also possible if humanity joins Satan in rebellion. In the Garden of Eden, the latter happens, and Satan has ostensibly won. But knowing the end from the beginning, God already has a plan to get humanity back to the perfect and sinless existence He intended for them when He placed them in the Garden of Eden. As He pronounces judgment upon Satan, He records for us His plan to send a man to deliver humanity from sin, death, and the archenemy. To the serpent, God says . . .

And I will put enmity between you and the woman, and between your seed and her seed; He shall bruise you on the head, and you shall bruise him on the heel (Genesis 3:15).

The struggle between Satan and people had only just begun. Satan would seed a race. Like Adam and Eve, created by God to be God's children, the descendants of Adam and Eve would have sin in their nature, making them—in a sense—children of the devil. They would still be made in "the image of God" (Genesis 1:26-28), but that image would be defaced (not erased) by the sin nature that would be inherited and by the sinful choices that would be made. But notice in Genesis 3:15 that Satan is not the only one who would have a seed; the woman would as well. Now, this is strange, because nowhere else in the Bible is a woman said to have a seed. Seed is everywhere else associated with men. But the man to whom this passage refers is no ordinary man.

Who is the only man in the history of the world (except the first Adam) to come into the world without the seed of a man? In other words, who is the only person ever born to a virgin? Every Christmas, the world pauses and replies to this question. We see Jesus "away in a manger", born to the Virgin Mary. Jesus alone gives meaning to this prediction of a "seed of the woman".

There are, in fact, three fascinating portrayals in Genesis 3:15 that reveal Jesus to be the unique *man*. First, as noted, He is born of a woman like any other man, but He is unique among men because He is conceived without the seed of a man. Second, the war between

Satan and humanity centers back upon *one* serpent and *one* man. Notice the singular pronouns. "*He* shall bruise *you* on the head, and *you* shall bruise *him* on the heel". Satan is clearly attempting to get at God by attacking God's image-bearing race—humanity. But *one* representative man is fighting on our behalf! The *one* virgin-born man holds the victory for all of humanity.

Finally, the wounds that Satan and the man inflict upon one another are astonishing. The serpent "shall bruise him on the heel". The man shall bruise the serpent "on the head". When Satan reared his ugly head in the Garden—blatantly contradicting God—God's vice-regent on earth (Adam was told to "rule . . . over every living thing that moves on the earth" Genesis 1:28) should have stomped out the deception. Adam should have crushed the Serpent's head! But since he instead submitted to the Serpent, God plans to send a second Adam to bring judgment on the Serpent. This man will strike Satan's head, but in the process receive a wound of his own. It is not only true that people kick at snakes and snakes bite at human heels. It would be trite to include such a little observation in this grand story that explains the entrance of sin and evil in the world.

No, this passage plays off of observable death wounds that people and snakes inflict upon each other, like a parable, in order to reveal the death wounds that Satan and the man would inflict upon each other. On the cross, the man—Christ Jesus—suffered a death wound as a stake was driven through His heel. On the cross, He defeated sin, death, and God's archenemy, dealing a death wound to Satan's head. The serpent struck the man's heel, but the man's heel crushed the serpent's head. As the narrative unfolds, so will the full meaning of Jesus' death be unveiled, but for now, we see the promise of a coming virgin-born "Seed of the woman"—*one man* who will receive a death wound to his heel but crush Satan's head in so doing.

King

Among all the living in 2000 BC, *Abraham* was selected to be first in a unique family tree. It is a family tree of a coming King who will bless the world (Genesis 12:1-3). Between Abraham's two sons, *Isaac* (and expressly not Ishmael) is the next generation selected to continue the lineage (Genesis 21:12). Next, although the older was usually preferred over the younger, Isaac's younger son *Jacob* receives the blessing instead of Esau (Genesis 25:23). The tree then branches out in 12 directions from Jacob because he has 12 sons, but again, only one will be selected among them.

In this way, Genesis zeroes in upon the King. The field of interpretation, the selected group of individuals who are eligible to be the King, narrows. As the number of humans grows throughout the earth, the percentage of those in the eligible group shrinks. In the penultimate chapter of Genesis, we learn which of the 12 sons of Jacob will receive the blessing of being a Patriarch to the coming King.

The Scepter will not depart from Judah, nor the ruler's staff from between his feet, until he to whom it belongs shall come and the obedience of the nations shall be his (Genesis 49:10).

Judah is selected and eleven twelfths of the Israelites are eliminated. At the time when Jesus came, Jewish people were far less than 1% of the world's population. But even within their tiny nation, 92% of them came from the wrong tribe to be the King. "The scepter will not depart from Judah". This prophecy reduces the sea of humanity to a mere pool in Israel—the Tribe of Judah—with regard to those who are fit to be King.

A thousand years after this man named Judah received this spoken prophecy, a shepherd boy belonging to the *Tribe of Judah* was anointed King of Israel. He was the famous King David. A thousand years after David, Mary and Joseph made their way to Bethlehem to register for a Roman Census because "they belonged to the house and line of David" (Luke 2:4). Among the animals in a stable, this humble woman from the *Tribe of Judah* gave birth to the King of Kings. "He to whom [the scepter] belongs" had come. The records of the genealogy of all Jewish people were kept in the Temple in Jerusalem. Consulting these, two witnesses (Matthew and Luke) wrote genealogical records of the ancestry of Jesus. These records are available to us today in their two books of the Bible. No other religious leader in history can match this claim. Ancient records show that Jesus is a descendant of Abraham, Isaac, Jacob, Judah, and David. It is therefore increasingly reasonable to conclude that He is the Christ—the promised one who was sent to rule and reign as the long-awaited King.

Priest

When he comes from heaven a second time, Christ will set up his Kingdom on earth. But the primary purpose of His first appearance was to serve as our *Priest*. A priest is a go-between—an intermediary—one who stands in the gap between a Holy God and sinful people. The primary problem that humanity faces is that we are sinners against a Holy God. We are separated from God on account of our sin. So, we need a Priest who can truly bridge that gap for us. We need someone who can offer the sacrifice that God requires and deliver the blessing that He gives.

Jesus is that Priest. His descent from Judah makes this hard to believe at first glance. As noted earlier, Jacob had 12 sons. The difficulty is that while Judah was chosen to establish the line of the coming *King*, Levi was chosen to establish a line of *priests*. How could Jesus be the final and Great High Priest if He doesn't descend from Levi? The answer is that while Isaac, Jacob and Levi were still only the coming seed of Abraham (before the descendants of Abraham were conceived), a different Priest appeared on the scene (Genesis 14:18-20). The Priesthood of which he was a part was a higher order than the one that would proceed from Abraham. We can know that this alternate Priesthood is superior to that which comes through Abraham because of a certain principle. It is a matter of principle, indeed it is consistent with the very nature of what *priesthood* is, that the lesser brings an offering to the greater, while the greater blesses the lesser. In the Genesis account, Abraham—the lesser—gives an offering to this Priest. The Priest—the greater—gives a blessing to Abraham.

And Melchizedek king of Salem brought out bread and wine; now he was a priest of God Most High. He blessed him and said, "Blessed be Abram of God Most High, Possessor of heaven and earth; and blessed be God Most High, who has delivered your enemies into your hand" (Genesis 14:18-20).

The mysterious Priest of Genesis 14 is superior to all the priests who descended from Abraham. This Superior Priest received a tenth of Abraham's possessions and delivered a blessing that only God could fulfill. He bridged the gap between Abraham and God. In so doing, he points us to Jesus Christ in five astonishing ways.

First, as noted above, he reveals how it is that Jesus could be the Great and Final High Priest even though Jesus is not a descendant from Levi—the Jewish tribe of Priests. As the Prophet-King David said, the Christ would be a Priest according to the "Order of Melchizedek" (Psalm 110:1-4). In the New Testament book of Hebrews, Jesus is specifically identified as being the Priest to which David referenced, "having become a high priest forever according to the order of Melchizedek" (Hebrews 6:20). The entire chapter seven of Hebrews goes on to delineate the parallels between Jesus and Melchizedek and the supremacy of Melchizedek's priesthood over Levi's. So first of all, Jesus is a Priest of a higher order than Levi and his descendants. Jesus is from the "Order of Melchizedek".

Second, the mysterious Priest's name—Melchizedek—means "Righteous King". We have shown that Jesus has the pedigree of a King because of his descent through Judah and David. As far as his righteousness is concerned, no one has ever shown even one instance where Jesus failed to be righteous. In fact, the Christian claim that Jesus was sinless would need to be true if indeed He was to serve as a Priest that could bring sinful people to a Holy God.

Third, this Priest hailed from Salem, a city whose name literally means "Peace". Jerusalem—the Peace of Jeru—was the City where Jesus served. Taken outside of her gates, He made the ultimate sacrifice and made *peace* between God and humanity.

Fourth, and this stands out strikingly because the words of the mysterious prophecy are so few, Melchizedek "brought out bread and wine" (Genesis 14:18). Anyone who has ever taken "Communion" will recognize the significance of what this Priest brings. On the night Jesus was betrayed, He took *bread* and broke it, saying, "this is my body, which is given for you" (1 Corinthians 11:24). He brought out *wine* and passed the cup, saying, "this is my blood of the covenant, which is poured out for many for the forgiveness of sins" (Matthew 26:28). Jesus the Priest brought the bread and wine of His own flesh and blood.

Fifth and finally, this Priest enters the Genesis narrative and exists as if he were from another world. He bursts onto the scene and then disappears, occupying but a couple of sentences in the text. Yet he accomplishes all of what has been said so far. Jesus, not of this world, but having come from eternity past at the right hand of His Father in heaven and having returned there, is without beginning or end. He appeared once—a Priest from heaven—to make a one-time sacrifice and bring sinners to a Holy God.

Sacrifice

In order to make atonement for the sins of people, priests bring *sacrifices* to God's altar, usually the blood of a bull, a goat, or a lamb. But the sacrifices prescribed by God in the Bible never sufficed to cleanse the guilty worshipper. This was for one simple reason. It is impossible for the blood of animals to take away human sin. Why then did God require sacrifices to be brought?

The first one to make a sacrifice was God Himself. After Adam and Eve sinned, they became ashamed of their nakedness. Shame was a part of their consequence for sin. But even within that fateful chapter (Genesis 3) where sin and death first infected humanity, there is a tangible expression of God's mercy. God kills an animal and makes coverings from its fur to clothe Adam and Eve (Genesis 3:21). The warmth and protection they receive comes on the other side of a horrible reminder of the severity of sin. "The wages of sin is death" (Romans 3:23). So, Adam and Eve needed to see death in order to understand what they had been spared. But there is an even more profound reason for the death of an animal and all the sacrificial blood offered in the 39 books of the Old Testament.

The sacrifices *pointed forward* to the shedding of Jesus' blood that would once and for all make atonement for the sins of the world. The animal sacrifices were *prophetic* in that they help us identify the Christ and understand what He came to do—namely to die upon the cross as a sacrifice for our sin. Whereas animal sacrifices could only make a covering for sin, the sacrifice of the body and blood of the God-Man could *take away* sin. His blood could wash away the stain of sin entirely. The priests who descended from Levi, who served at an altar in the Temple, offered sacrifices that demonstrated the horror of sin and served as placeholders until the true sacrifice was made for humankind. The Priest who appeared from heaven, whose own body was a Temple that held the very Presence of God, offered the

Sacrifice of His own body and blood. Jesus was not only a Priest; He was the Lamb being slaughtered.

This reality is the heart of the Gospel message. It is the core proposition that makes Christianity. What happened on that cross in 33AD to that God-Man Priest-King named Jesus is what saves sinners from eternal death. He became God's sacrifice. Those who believe that Jesus is the Christ, that He died for our sins, that He arose from the dead, will not be separated from God forever. Their sins will be forgiven. So God gave ample testimony to the reality of this core proposition. It is His desire that each of us would believe and that none would be lost.

The clearest prophetic picture of Jesus' *sacrifice* in the book of Genesis appears in chapter 22. In the passage, God tests Abraham's faith. We could all learn about faith based on Abraham's response. But the passage has a deeper level of meaning that commends faith in Jesus Christ.

Now it came about after these things, that God tested Abraham, and said to him, "Abraham!" And he said, "Here I am." He said, "Take now your son, your only son, whom you love, Isaac, and go to the land of Moriah, and offer him there as a burnt offering on one of the mountains of which I will tell you." So Abraham rose early in the morning and saddled his donkey, and took two of his young men with him and Isaac his son; and he split wood for the burnt offering, and arose and went to the place of which God had told him. On the third day Abraham raised his eyes and saw the place from a distance. Abraham said to his young men, "stay here with the donkey, and I and the lad will go over there; and we will worship and return to you." Abraham took the wood of the burnt offering and laid it on Isaac his son, and he took in his hand the fire and the knife. So the two of them walked on together. Isaac spoke to Abraham his father and said, "My father!" And he said, "Here I am, my son." And he said, "Behold, the fire and the wood, but where is the lamb for the burnt offering?" Abraham said, "God will provide for Himself the lamb for the burnt offering, my son." So the two of them walked on together. Then they came to the place of which God had told him; and Abraham built the altar there and arranged the wood, and bound his son Isaac and laid him on the altar, on top of the wood. Abraham stretched out his hand and took the knife to slay his son. But the angel of the Lord called to him from heaven and said, "Abraham, Abraham!" And he said, "Here I am." He said, "Do not stretch out your hand against the lad, and do nothing to him; for now I know that you fear God, since you have not withheld your son, your only son, from Me." Then Abraham raised his eyes and looked, and behold, behind him a ram caught in the thicket by his horns; and Abraham went and took the ram and offered him up for a burnt offering in the place of his son. Abraham called the name of that place The Lord Will Provide, as it is said to this day, "In the mount of the Lord it will be provided" (Genesis 22:1-14).

There are **eight** clear ways that this passage foreshadows the sacrifice of Jesus Christ:

First, it concerns a *Father* and his unique *Son* of promise. The chapters that precede this one reveal how special Isaac is. Similarly, the Bible will reveal God as a Father and Jesus as the unique Son.

Second, the Father must *sacrifice* his Son. People often ask who killed Jesus. The best answer is to say that the Father did, "for God so loved the world that *He gave* His one and only Son…" (John 3:16).

Third, Abraham's son Isaac goes *willingly* and lies down to be sacrificed. As Jesus said about His own life, "no one has taken it away from Me, but I lay it down on My own initiative" (John 10:18).

Fourth, the sacrificial son rides into the area on a donkey. Jesus entered Jerusalem riding on a donkey before being led away to be slaughtered like a lamb.

Fifth, the sacrificial son must climb a *mountain* to provide the sacrifice. As Genesis 22:14 says, "on the mountain of the Lord it will be provided". Jesus climbed Mount Calvary to die for us.

Sixth, the one to die must carry the *wood* of his sacrifice. As confused Isaac shouldered the load (Genesis 22:7), so the true sacrifice bore the weight of the wooden cross on the way to Calvary.

Seventh, a *substitute* is provided for Isaac at the last second, another ram (Genesis 22:13) to mark the place of the Christ until He comes. No substitute would be provided for Jesus. It was not possible (Matthew 26:39) because He alone would be the substitute that would die in the place of sinners. The sinless one took the penalty for sinners like Abraham and Isaac, you and I.

Eighth and finally, Abraham expected to receive Isaac *back from the dead*, raised to life by the power of God (Hebrews 11:17-19). He did receive Isaac back from death in a figurative sense, because God did not make him go through with the sacrifice. But this again points forward to the One who literally died, and behold, He lives!

The Full Weight of the Prophecies

Any one of my interpretations of the prophecies we are discussing could be written off as a biased attempt by a Christian to justify his preconceived conclusions. One could chalk it up to chance or an agenda I have to "make it fit". But the full weight of what is objectively recorded in Genesis crushes any human desire to write off the predictive elements of what God has written. I agree that human beings are not neutral. We all have agendas and preconceptions that we wish to justify. The root of this self-justifying is pride, the source of which is revealed in Genesis 3. Sin is a part of our nature. So if you find yourself bent on denying what is plainly revealed, then question your preconceptions. Do you have an agenda that keeps you from believing in Jesus Christ? The prophecies of Genesis pile up and crush our unbelief.

Genesis inspires faith in Jesus Christ. **God** is one, but introduces Himself to humanity as a plurality—"Elohim" (1:1) and let "us" make man in "our" image (1:26). A "Seed of the woman"—one **Man**, not many—will crush the head of the serpent while being struck in the heel (3:15). The **King** who is coming will descend from Abraham (12:1-3), Isaac (21:12), Jacob (25:23) and Judah (49:10). The **Priest** who makes peace between sinful humanity and a Holy God will be like Melchizedek (14:18-20)—no beginning or end, from the city of Peace, a Righteous King, bringing bread and wine. The **Sacrifice** is not an animal, but a unique Son who rides in on a donkey, then climbs a mountain as He shoulders the wood upon which He is to die, willingly lies down upon it, substitutes His life for ours, and rises from the dead. Jesus alone fits the description of the God-Man-King-Priest-Sacrifice that the Book of Genesis prophesied about. Jesus is the Christ, the Son of the Living God.

CHAPTER 2

SEEN IN THE SAVIOR: *EXODUS*

The second book of the Bible, like the first, is filled with familiar stories. Exodus tells how the Israelites were harshly treated as slaves in Egypt, how God sent Moses to demand that Pharaoh would "let My people go", how God sent ten plagues to break Pharaoh's stubborn resistance, and how God delivered and protected His people. As in Genesis, we find amazing clues within the narrative concerning the One that God promised to send to save us from our sins. Genesis clued us in to the fact that the Christ would be *God, Man, King, Priest, and Sacrifice.* Exodus adds even more detail to the picture. Whereas Genesis gave us a *Title* for God—Elohim—by which we came to expect Plurality within the Unity of who God is, Exodus gives us a *Name* for God—Yahweh—by which the God of Israel can be distinguished from all that are falsely called Deity.

Like Genesis, Exodus will paint a picture of Christ using the color *red.* The blood of lambs will be the key that unlocks Israel's deliverance from Egypt. Later on, the blood of Jesus will be required in order to set us free—not from slavery to men, but from slavery to sin. So, the picture of Jesus becomes clearer. Exodus leaves the world waiting for *Yahweh* to send a *Savior* to deliver His people by the *blood of the Passover Lamb.*

Yahweh

The various religions of the world do *not* all worship the same God. When God sent ten plagues upon Egypt, each one directly challenged the false conceptions of the Egyptians. They worshipped the sun. God blocked it out for a time. They worshipped frogs. God swarmed the land with them. They worshipped the Nile. God turned it into blood. Even in the areas outside of Egypt, people worshipped a variety of false gods. In the Arabian Desert, people worshipped the moon god—Al-Ilah Sin, which was also represented by a calf. So when Moses saw a burning bush in the desert that miraculously wasn't being consumed, he needed to know which God was producing this strange manifestation.

In reality, there has only ever been one true God. But just as in the present day, people in Moses' day held a wide variety of misconceptions. Standing on holy ground, Moses wanted to know God's Name, not just a generic title like "God". "If the Israelites ask, 'What is His Name?'", Moses asked, "What shall I say?" God's reply was crucial:

God said to Moses, "I AM WHO I AM"; and He said, "Thus you shall say to the sons of Israel, 'I AM has sent me to you.'" God, furthermore, said to Moses, "Thus you shall say to the sons of Israel, 'The Lord, the God of your fathers, the God of Abraham, the God of Isaac, and the God of Jacob, has sent me to you.' This is My name forever, and this is My memorial-name to all generations (Exodus 3:14-15).

The name YAHWEH, a Hebrew derivation of I AM WHO I AM, is more than a title. It is not simply God, Elohim, Allah, gods, or another general term that anyone can use to refer to their conception of Deity. Rather, it is a Name from the Book of Exodus that the God of Abraham, Isaac, Jacob, and Moses ascribed to Himself. It carries within it all the force of an eternally existent, utterly independent, reality-defining Creator of all that exists outside of Himself. It is very specific to Himself—over and against any other so-called "god". It is very meaningful, descriptive of an ultimate Reality, not a part of this creation.

When Jesus appeared, He made **seven** statements that the Jewish leaders took as blasphemy. Indeed they should have been offended, that is, had the statements not been true. Very few in the history of the world have made claims like these, and the others who did were either devils or deluded. But understanding Exodus 3:14-15, one is able to grasp why Jesus' claims were so profound. He is not only describing Himself with analogies that would only apply to God ("Bread of Life", "Light of the World", etc.), He begins each claim with the Memorial-Name of God—"I AM".

1. I AM the Bread of Life (John 6:48)
2. I AM the Light of the World (John 8:12)
3. I AM the Door (John 10:9)
4. I AM the Good Shepherd (John 10:11)
5. I AM the Resurrection and the Life (John 11:25)

6. I AM the Way, the Truth, and the Life (John 14:6)
7. I AM the True Vine (John 15:1)

When taken in context, it is impossible to escape the force of what Jesus claims about Himself. He claims to be the Source of all life. By coming to Him, those who are wandering in the dark are able to enter into the Father's house. Jesus even claims to be able to raise the dead unto everlasting life! What's even more, He claims "no one comes to the Father *except* by Me" (John 14:6), so the road to eternal life is *exclusively* His.

When the Jews pick up stones to kill Him for these remarks, He doubles down with an even clearer assertion of His Deity. "Before Abraham was even born, I AM" (John 8:58). Jesus makes His claim to be God explicit with these words. No ordinary man predates his own father. But Jesus says that He even predates the father of the nation. Given what every Israelite knew about God's Name and Exodus 3:14-15, they understood perfectly well that Jesus was saying that His was the Voice from the burning bush. Moses encountered the God of Abraham, Isaac and Jacob that day long ago, but even before that . . . I AM WHO I AM.

The Jews didn't miss what Jesus was saying. In fact, God had made sure no one would have an excuse for misunderstanding. *I AM* is God's "name forever, and this is My memorial-name to all generations" (Exodus 3:15). The Book of Exodus provided the Name of God, Yahweh—I AM—in order that no one would be able to mistake Jesus' claim for anything less than an absolute assertion that He is God. Jesus thus left us no option but to conclude that He is either a liar, a lunatic, or the Lord He claims to be.

Savior

Moses is a *type* of the Savior. Before Jesus came as the Savior of the world, God sent Moses to prefigure Him, so that when Jesus came, we would recognize God's pattern and accept Jesus as genuine. The similarities between Moses and Jesus are striking. The real difference between them is that Moses' life was only a foreshadowing that God used in order to deliver a relatively small portion of humanity from one grave circumstance, while Jesus is the true God and Savior of all.

Fifteen parallels between Moses and Jesus provide strong evidence that God was at work validating the claim that Jesus is the Savior of the world.

1. Like Jesus, Moses was born under the reign of a psychotic ruler who enslaved Israel and ruthlessly murdered Hebrew baby boys.
2. Both were hidden in Egypt.
3. Both humbled themselves, abstaining from the lavish lifestyle that was available to the sons of kings.
4. Moses became the leading human figure of the Old Testament and Jesus of the New Testament.
5. Both fasted 40 days.
6. God used Moses to turn water into blood. Jesus turned water into wine.
7. Moses sent out 12 spies. Jesus sent 12 disciples.
8. Both also appointed 70 for a mission.

9. God divided the waters for Moses to walk through. Jesus walked upon the waters.
10. God fed Moses and thousands of people with Manna. Jesus fed 5000 by a creative miracle from his own hand.
11. Both showed compassion to a woman drawing water at a well.
12. Both would die upon a mountain.
13. Moses lifted up the bronze serpent on a pole for Israel's healing, while Jesus was Himself lifted up on a cross for the healing of all who would look to Him in faith.
14. Moses brought water out of a rock. Jesus brought forth water from his side.
15. Both lead their people to the Promised Land, but Jesus to an eternal inheritance kept securely in heaven for His children.

The full list of striking similarities is at least fifty in number. The fifteen mentioned here constitute almost conclusive proof of Divine intervention in the construction of the Christian Bible in its Old and New Testaments. That the Bible is special revelation from God is the best explanation for the parallels. If someone tried to explain away the shadows of Jesus that appear in Moses' life, he or she might find some limited success, that is, if they limited themselves to explaining away only a few of them. But the cumulative weight of all fifty, or even fifteen, is overwhelming. Each of these events was very unusual. Look back over the list of fifteen. Would any of the fifteen apply to the events in your own life or anyone you know?

Moses himself instructed Israel to wait for a prophet who was like him (Deuteronomy 18:15, 18). Jesus is that promised one, for the fifteen reasons given and because of the amazing parallel between the missions of Moses and Jesus. Even as Israel was enslaved under cruel taskmasters, so are we enslaved by sin. We, like them, desperately need a Savior, because we are helpless to save ourselves. Our only hope was that God would send a Savior. God knew this, and 1500 years before He sent Jesus Christ, God gave us a Type of the Savior—Moses—so that when the time arrived to send Jesus, we would trust Him as our Savior.

Passover Lamb

How does The Savior save? He offers sacrificial blood to atone for sin. The reason that blood must be shed is to administer the penalty for sin. God is rich in mercy and desires to forgive sin. But He is also just, so He rightly desires to judge rebellion. He brought together His love and justice by allowing the death of a substitute to stand in the place of guilty people. But what could stand as a worthy substitute in place of all people? Surely a bull, goat, or lamb could not do it. Neither could an ordinary man, since he is only a part of this creation.

To be sure, a man must die in order to reconcile men to God. But it is God Himself who must absorb the pain of sacrifice. He cannot simply substitute something else that He made to die in the place of human beings. Before the world began, God the Father determined to lay the penalty of human sin upon God the Son. Jesus would take on human flesh and die the death that we deserve. Jesus would be an infinitely valuable substitute to die in place of sinful humans. Since this was God's plan from the beginning, He made the blood of lambs the key to Israel's deliverance from Egypt, because the blood of lambs would point the world to the blood of Jesus.

Nine devastating plagues did not break the Israelites free. The tenth plague—an angel of death to kill every firstborn in Egypt—was about to be unleashed. But the Israelites deserved to die just as much as the Egyptians did! "All have sinned and fall short of the glory of God" (Romans 3:23). Even Moses—Israel's "savior"—was also a murderer. How could Israel be spared from the angel of death?

Israel was instructed to sacrifice lambs, drain their blood into bowls, and use the blood to paint the doorframes of their homes. That night, a night that would forever be remembered as the Jewish "Passover", the angel of death moved throughout all of Egypt and killed every firstborn, animal and human alike. But when he came to a house marked with blood, he passed over. Those families who trusted God and His provision of the blood of a lamb were saved from death.

Your lamb shall be an unblemished male . . . the whole assembly of the congregation of Israel is to kill it at twilight. Moreover they shall take some of the blood and put it on the two doorposts and on the lintel of the houses in which they eat. They shall eat the flesh that same night, roasted with fire, and they shall eat it with unleavened bread and bitter herbs (Exodus 12:5-8).

The Passover Lamb is a picture of Jesus Christ:

First, Jesus was like a Lamb in that He went without objection to be slaughtered.

Second, Jesus was unblemished. If He had ever sinned, then He would have needed to die for His own sins. But as a perfect Man, He could be substituted for sinful men.

Third, Jesus died during the Passover Festival. The congregation of Israel came out together in 33AD to shout "Crucify! Crucify!" at the Passover Lamb. It was no coincidence that Jesus was killed during the Passover Festival. And it was no coincidence that Israel remembered the Passover, faithfully celebrating it for 1500 years until the time for the true Passover sacrifice had fully come.

Fourth, it was blood that stood between the Israelites and the death they deserved. In the same way, only the blood of Jesus interposes between the Righteous Judge and the guilty sinner.

Fifth, the wood of the doorframes represents the wooden beams of the cross. The crown of thorns drew blood and marked the top of the cross, symbolized by the lintel. Spikes driven through the wrists of Jesus soaked the outer sides of the cross and streamed down, symbolized by the marks down the doorposts. Although the Israelites could only see a shadow of the real thing, Jesus was hung up between them and death in order to keep them safe.

Sixth, the Israelites were instructed to eat the Lamb. "So Jesus said to them, 'Truly, truly, I say to you, unless you eat the flesh of the Son of Man and drink His blood, you have no life in yourselves" (John 6:53).

Seventh, the Israelites were also instructed to eat "unleavened bread and bitter herbs". Jesus' body was unleavened, meaning that He had no sin. Yeast spreads and works its way through dough. But Jesus was free from even the slightest taint of sin. He ate the bitter herbs of crucifixion on our behalf. The night before Jesus was sacrificed as the Passover Lamb, Jesus instructed us to remember Him. "The Lord Jesus in the night in which He was betrayed took bread; and when He had given thanks, He broke it and said, 'This is My body, which is for you; do this in remembrance of Me" (1 Corinthians 11:23-24).

The Full Weight of the Prophecies

The Book of Exodus provides profound reasons to believe in Jesus Christ. Time does not permit us to explore every way in which His life mirrored that of Moses. But we make note of what Moses said. "The Lord your God will raise up for you a prophet *like me* from among you, from your countrymen, you shall listen to him" (Deuteronomy 18:15). Jesus fit the bill far more precisely than anyone else in the history of the world. But what did Jesus say, to which we are instructed to listen? He claimed to be **Yahweh**! "I AM the Resurrection and the Life." "I AM the way, the truth, and the life." I AM WHO I AM.

So why was the God of the Universe dwelling among us in human flesh? He came as a **Savior** for all humanity. He came to die as the unblemished **Passover Lamb**, sparing us from the penalty of death that we deserve on account of our sins. Jesus placed His blood in position between guilty sinners and the wrath of a Holy God.

CHAPTER 3

SEEN IN THE BLOOD
LEVITICUS

Leviticus is the skeptic's favorite book of the Bible to quote. It is used more often than any to deride the Christian claim that the Bible is the authoritative Word of God: "If you are going to take the Bible literally, then why don't you go ahead and call for homosexuals to be killed, since you say they cannot marry. Leviticus 20:13 says, 'If there is a man who lies with a male as those who lie with a woman, both of them have committed a detestable act; they shall surely be put to death. Their blood-guiltiness is upon them.' It also says you can't trim your beard, cut your hair at the sides, get tattoos, or sell land permanently. Do you do any of those?"

The accusation is that Christians cherry-pick laws for the purpose of condemning others and hypocritically ignore the ones we want to break. But is it wise for skeptics to take verses they don't like and interpret them out of context in order to justify their preconceived conclusion that the Bible is not the Word of God?

The simple truth is that Christians are not under the Law of Moses, of which the laws found in Leviticus are a part. Time will not permit us to explore Exodus 24 in depth. If we did, we would see how even it points to Jesus Christ. But it is important to note that in that chapter, God initiated a Covenant between Himself and Israel, and the terms of that contract were up to Him. That Covenant—or agreement—is referred to as the Law of Moses. God had every right to write the Law, and He even asked Israel to give it their consent. God didn't owe that much to Israel, but He did request their agreement, which they gave. So who are we to question how He chose to regulate their diet, their morality, their dress code, their haircuts, and the system of sacrifices that He required them to bring? He had the right to prescribe penalties for lawbreakers. A modern reader may not like the terms of God's Covenant with Israel, but who is he or she to stand in judgment over God?

What the skeptic misses is that God provided the Book of Leviticus for our instruction *even though we do not live under the terms of the Covenant.* Our Covenant was not initiated in Exodus 24 but with the bloody death of Jesus Christ. As He said, "This cup which is poured out for you is the *new covenant* in My blood" (Luke 22:20). Skeptics claim that this is all-too-convenient. But it is entirely consistent with the plan God spoke about all along. "Behold, days are coming', declares the Lord, 'when I will make a *new covenant* with the house of Israel and the house of Judah, not like the covenant which I made with their fathers in the day I took them by the hand to bring them out of the land of Egypt, My covenant which they broke, although I was a husband to them,' declares the Lord" (Jeremiah 31:31-32).

The purpose of the Old Covenant was to make humanity conscious of our sin and our helpless state. The Old Covenant left us aware of our need for a Savior. And it pointed to Jesus, so that we would recognize Him at His appearing. The skeptic scoffs at a law that forbids eating meat cooked too rare, but even this law was a tutor to bring us to Christ, if we allow ourselves to be taught by God rather than standing in judgment upon Him:

And any man from the house of Israel, or from the aliens who sojourn among them, who eats any blood, I will set My face against that person who eats blood and will cut him off from among the people. For the life of the flesh is in the blood, and I have given it to you on the altar to make atonement for your souls; for it is the blood by reason of the life that makes atonement. Therefore I said to the sons of Israel, "No person among you may eat blood, nor may any alien who sojourns among you eat blood" (Leviticus 17:10-12).

When God initiated the Covenants—Old and New He did so with the sprinkling of *blood. Blood* is very prominent in Leviticus. The Book of *Leviticus* specifies regulations for the Priests of Israel—the *Levites.* The primary job of the Levites was to offer *blood* sacrifices upon the altar of God. Once a year on the "Day of Atonement", the High Priest went into the Most Holy Place and offered *blood* upon the Mercy Seat. Even on a daily basis, a rotation of priests shed the *blood* of animals on an altar on behalf of worshipers. "And according to the Law, one may almost say, all things are cleansed with *blood*, and without shedding of *blood* there is no forgiveness" (Hebrews 9:22).

Leviticus 17:11 is not an arbitrary law. It explains that *life is in the blood*, so blood was required to atone for sins. The life of an animal was accepted in place of the worshiper's own life. The guilty sinner would stand by and watch a death penalty be administered to an animal that stood in his or her place. We may have an impulse to pull away from the gruesome imagery, but like the ancient Israelites, we also need to face the severity of our sin. Sin is gruesome. It is rebellion against the All-powerful Creator whose eyes are too pure to look upon evil and do nothing. So, we must look to Jesus and consider the cross and His blood.

The blood of Jesus—His life—was offered once for all. The Book of Leviticus instructs us that the Levites stood "daily ministering and offering time after time the same sacrifices, which can never take away sin; but He, having offered one sacrifice for sins for all time sat down at the right hand of God" (Hebrews 10:11-12). As we learned in the chapter on Genesis, Jesus was not a Levite. He was the Priest of a higher order. If the Bible is God's special revelation, then we would expect the development of themes—layer upon layer of developing complexity—but also simple consistency.

This is precisely what we have. By developing the theme of Israel's sacrificial system and showing how blood is required to make atonement for sin—life is in the blood—the Book of Leviticus continues to drive us toward faith in Jesus Christ. It is unwise to mock that which we do not understand. But it is vital to understand at least this one thing from the Book of Leviticus: Life is in the blood of Jesus and God has given it to make atonement for our souls.

CHAPTER 4

SEEN IN THE RAISED SERPENT
NUMBERS

Even someone who is unfamiliar with the Book of Numbers can no doubt guess one thing that we are sure to find there. We will surely find a lot of numbers. But like the three books of the Bible that went before it and like the thirty-five that follow, there is another thing that we are sure to find in the Book of Numbers. We will surely find prophecies about the coming Messiah. As demonstrated in Genesis, Exodus, and Leviticus, there is no need to force it, to try to make something fit. The force of what we've already seen to this point in Scripture is overwhelming. There is plurality (Elohim) within the unity of God. You will recognize His memorial-name, I AM WHO I AM. The seed of the woman will be struck in the heel, but crush the head of the serpent. The king who will bless the whole world will descend from Abraham, Isaac, Jacob, and Judah. He will save His people from slavery, bearing resemblance to Moses. The priest will not be a Levite, but be like Melchizedek. His sacrifice will be a

Passover Lamb, sparing people of faith from eternal death.

The Lamb is Jesus. The blood He offers is His own. When you picture Jesus upon the cross, remember the Passover blood on the lintel and doorposts. Recall Isaac lying down upon the wood, ready to die upon the mountain. See that substitute caught in the thicket nearby. Don't forget the priests cleansing nearly everything with blood. Consider that life is in the blood of Jesus and that all these things were written in order that we would believe He made atonement for our souls when He died on the cross.

The Book of Numbers provides data about how many troops each tribe of Israel had, but it also provides still further reason to believe in the King of Kings. Numbers 24:17 reminds us that a "Scepter shall rise out of Israel" and connects that Ruler with another analogy that describes no ordinary man: "there shall come a Star out of Jacob". Befitting Hebrew parallelism, Jacob is another name for Israel and *the Scepter is the Star*. The King is a consuming Fire, a glorious Light, a rising Beacon of God's glory. Numbers provides this wonderful image of the King, but it also provides the most horrifying image of Him in the Bible, a serpent.

On the other side of the horror, the most wonderful verse in the Bible emerges. The best-known verse in the Bible is John 3:16, but John 3:14-15 was necessary to get us there.

As Moses lifted up the serpent in the wilderness, even so must the Son of Man be lifted up; so that whoever believes will in Him have eternal life. For God so loved the world, that He gave His only begotten Son, that whoever believes in Him shall not perish, but have eternal life (John 3:14-16).

In order to understand why believers in Jesus are given eternal life, one must understand what happened when Jesus was "lifted up". The image presented to us is that of "the serpent in the wilderness". It is there in order to help our understanding of what Jesus did on the cross. How is Jesus like this serpent?

The people spoke against God and Moses . . . The Lord sent fiery serpents among the people and they bit the people, so that many people of Israel died. So the people came to Moses and said, "we have sinned . . ." Then the Lord said to Moses, "Make a fiery serpent, and set it on a standard; and it shall come about, that everyone who is bitten, when he looks at it, he will live" (Numbers 21:5-8).

The *serpent theme* began in the Garden of Eden. Satan in the form of a serpent tempts Adam and Eve, and they bring sin into humanity by submitting to his temptation. Humankind has suffered a death wound. As God warned Adam, "In the day that you eat from it, you will surely die" (Genesis 2:17). But mercifully, God delayed physical death and instead promised to reverse the curse. God promised to send a "seed of the woman" who would crush the head of the serpent. In so doing, this seed of the woman would also suffer a death wound, being struck in his heel. So we see that the serpent is symbolic of the curse of sin, evil, and death that has come upon humanity. Humanity is longing for a Savior to come and break the curse.

The horrifying image presented in Numbers is that the promised Deliverer must, in a sense, *become sin* as He stands in the place of sinners to bear their punishment. The New Testament explains it best. God "made Him who knew no sin to be sin on our behalf, so that we might become the righteousness of God in Him" (2 Corinthians 5:21). This is the key to understanding the Gospel. Most people in America can tell you that "Jesus died on the cross for our sins", but not half of them can tell you what that means. That Jesus died *for our sins* means that He allowed Himself to be punished as if all the filth of our rebellion, all the evil in our hearts, all the sin of humankind was *His* doing and part of *His* nature. He took our sin upon Himself and died in our place. That is why Moses lifted up a Serpent on a pole.

The serpent was an image that represented the curse of sin, evil, and death that plagues humanity. Suspending that bronze image up toward heaven was a picture of the sun-scorched body of Jesus being lifted up on the cross, becoming sin on our behalf. When Jesus hung on the cross, the Father turned His face away. He allowed His Son to suffer in our stead. The Roman Governor said, "I find no fault in this man" (John 19:6). The guilty man on the cross next to Jesus saw that Jesus didn't belong next to him. "We are punished justly, for we are getting what our deeds deserve. But this man has done nothing wrong" (Luke 23:41). They were right, and that is the point. Jesus was an innocent Lamb, but He allowed Himself to be treated as if He were hell's serpent.

There is only one remedy for us. It is the same call that Moses gave the Israelites. It is so simple. It requires nothing from us except that we trust God, taking Him at His word. It destroys any hope we have in our efforts to earn righteousness by being good enough. It completely humbles us. We must recognize that the snake bit us too.

We are dying, and it is only a matter of time before our bodies return to the ground and our souls depart from God forever. If we do this one thing, then we too will be healed. The promise seems too big, but God's mercy is just that big. "Everyone who is bitten, when he looks at it, he will live" (Numbers 21:8). *"As Moses lifted up the serpent in the wilderness, even so must the Son of Man be lifted up; so that whoever believes will in Him have eternal life" (John 3:14-15).* Look at Jesus, hanging upon the cross, having become sin for you. Simply believe in Him.

CHAPTER 5

SEEN IN THE GREATER PROPHET

DEUTERONOMY

"Deutero" means *second* and "nomy" denotes *law*, so this fifth book of the Bible and final Book of Moses is a reiteration of the Law as found in Exodus, Leviticus, and Numbers. Deuteronomy renews the Covenant. It tells Israel what blessings will come upon them when they obey it and what curses will befall them when they don't. Moses has brought them to the edge of the Promised Land, but he is not the one to bring them in. Even though Moses was a great prophet, God says, "because you did not uphold my holiness among the Israelites, therefore you will see the land only from a distance; you will not enter the land I am giving to the people of Israel" (Deuteronomy 32:51-52). It was time for Moses to die. He fulfilled his purpose in his time, and that purpose was chiefly to reveal a Prophet who was even greater than him. Moses was a great prophet, but not as great as the one to come. Whoever wrote the addendum to the Book of Deuteronomy commented appropriately.

Since then, no prophet has risen in Israel like Moses, whom the Lord knew face to face, who did all those miraculous signs and wonders the Lord sent him to do in Egypt—to Pharaoh and to all his officials and to his whole land. For no one has ever shown the mighty power or performed the awesome deeds that Moses did in the sight of all Israel (Deuteronomy 34:10-12).

Enter Jesus Christ. He is a greater Prophet who brings a greater Covenant. The miracles He will perform will validate Him as the greatest prophet, who far-surpasses even Moses. The miracles of Jesus reveal that He is a Prophet and More-than-a-Prophet. Moses performed miracles with a staff in his hand—the rod of God—in order to remind him and all Israel that God was working the miracles and Moses was only an instrument in God's hand. But Jesus' own hands created bread and fish to feed thousands of people on more than one occasion. Jesus raised His own hand and told a hurricane, "quiet, be still" (Mark 4:39). With absolute command over nature, He spoke, "and the wind died down, and it became perfectly calm" (Mark 4:39). He did not need a rod of God to touch the waters of the Sea and divide them. Jesus is God, so He simply walked upon them.

The miracles of Jesus revealed that He was more than a Prophet. His miracles were an outworking of His Deity. Jesus said that his miracles prove that He can do what only God can do—take away sins. The New Covenant promised the forgiveness of sin. The miracles of the Greater Prophet proved that He speaks for God in the things He promised.

Knowing their thoughts, Jesus said, "Why do you entertain evil thoughts in your hearts? Which is easier: to say, 'your sins are forgiven,' or to say, 'Get up and walk'? But so that you may know that the Son of Man has authority on earth to forgive sins . . ." Then he said to the paralytic, "Get up, take your mat and go home." And the man got up and went home (Matthew 9:4-7).

It is imperative that we listen to everything that Jesus says. There is a terrible disconnect that often emerges as people talk about Jesus today. They happily say, "Oh, I have the highest respect for Jesus. He was a great prophet!" Muslims esteem Him as one of the greatest prophets. Many others do as well, and rightly so. But what does a prophet do? A prophet speaks for God. When God promised a prophet greater than Moses, He underscored the importance of listening to the actual words of the prophet, not just acknowledging that he is one.

I will raise up a prophet from among their countrymen like you, and I will put my words in his mouth, and he shall speak to them all that I command him. It shall come about that whoever will not listen to my words which he shall speak in my name, I myself will require it of him (Deuteronomy 18:18-19).

In studying Exodus, we saw fifteen ways in which Jesus was similar to Moses, fulfilling the "like you" aspect of this Deuteronomy prophecy. But notice here that the words of this coming prophet, who turns out to be Jesus, are said to carry absolute authority. God the Father says, "whoever will not listen to *My* words which *He* shall speak in *My* name, *I Myself* will require it of him". The words that Jesus speaks are the very words of the Father. Those who accept His testimony are saved, but those who reject Him are actually rejecting the Father as well. So what did Jesus say?

For God did not send His Son into the world to condemn the world, but to save the world through Him. Whoever believes in Him is not condemned, but whoever does not believe stands condemned already because he has not believed in the Name of God's one and only Son (John 3:17-18).

These are the actual words of the Prophet. What does He say that we must not ignore? He professes certain things about Himself. He claims to be the Son of God. The most important thing to remember when calling Jesus a Prophet is that His words carry God's authority and His words proclaim Himself to be equal with God the Father. There is a logical disconnect when someone says that Jesus was a prophet but not the Son of God. If He was the former, then He must have been the latter. In the above passage alone, the Prophet 1) calls Himself the Son of God, 2) says He was sent by God to save the world, and 3) pronounces condemnation upon anyone who persists in unbelief until the end. Such an authoritative claim does not appear in a vacuum. Jesus simply echoes what the Father said. "I myself will require it of him" who does not listen to the Prophet's words.

Prophecy can be either "forth-telling", as in proclaiming what is true, or "fore-telling", as in predicting future events. Jesus was a prophet in both senses of the word. At a time when there were only a few hundred followers of Jesus Christ, and they had never travelled outside of that tiny sliver of land that is Israel, Jesus foretold the following.

And this Gospel of the kingdom will be preached in the whole world as a testimony to all nations, and then the end will come (Matthew 24:14).

This prophecy is being fulfilled in our generation as Christian missionaries penetrate the last of the unreached places on Planet Earth. The spread of Christianity over the last 2000 years is a marvel to modern sociologists. But to the Prophet Jesus, it was the inevitable course of history. The Prophet saw the end from the beginning. But unlike any other prophet, Jesus *is* the Beginning and the End. As He said, "I am the Alpha and the Omega…who is, and who was, and who is to come, the Almighty" (Revelation 1:8). The main thing that Jesus prophesied was concerning His own person. In fact, the main purpose of all prophecy is the exaltation of Jesus. "For the testimony of Jesus is the spirit of prophecy" (Revelation 19:10). We would do well to heed the actual words of the prophet. Jesus said, "He who has believed and has been baptized shall be saved; but he who has disbelieved shall be condemned" (Mark 16:16).

CHAPTER 6

SEEN IN THE CAPTAIN
JOSHUA

It is not hard to find Christ in the sixth book of the Bible. The book was named after Him. *Joshua*—Yehoshu'a in Hebrew—comes into the English language as *Jesus.* The name is a perfect descriptor of who He is. It literally means "Yahweh is salvation", so the essence of the Gospel is in the Name. The Gospel is the person and work of the Christ. His person is who He is, Yahweh I AM WHO I AM. His work is saving sinners. *Yahweh is salvation.* Peter said it simply in Acts 4:12, "there is salvation in no one else; for there is no other name under heaven that has been given among men by which we must be saved". Is it a coincidence that the first book of the Bible named after a person is "Joshua"? Or was the Bible given to reveal Jesus?

Salvation has two elements. When someone is *saved*, there is something that is taken away, and there is something that is given. One cannot have one element without the other. They are like two sides of the same coin. Salvation is 1) being *forgiven* of sin and 2) being *given* eternal life. When God brought Israel out of captivity in Egypt, this event pictured our deliverance from sin. Our Savior came to set us free from the penalty of sin. We were slaves to sin because there was nothing we could do to break the chains of the penalty that was hanging over our heads. But Israel was not only set free from something, she was given something. Not only was she taken out of Egypt, she was brought into the Promised Land. The Book of Joshua pictures the completeness of salvation that we have in Jesus Christ. "Therefore He is also able to save forever those who draw near to God through Him" (Hebrews 7:25).

The Promised Land represents eternal life. When a person accepts Christ, the reality is that all sin is immediately forgiven and eternal life has immediately begun. However, there is also a process of *taking hold of the life* that was given. When someone gets saved, they must learn to walk in the newness of life that belongs to them. They need to mature in their new life, much as a baby must grow up. The New Testament gives much instruction, such as the following, that teaches us how to take hold of our new life, how to experience the fullness of what life is all about:

Instruct those who are rich in this present world not to be conceited or to fix their hope on the uncertainty of riches, but on God, who richly supplies us with all things to enjoy. Instruct them to do good, to be rich in good works, to be generous and ready to share, storing up for themselves the treasure of a good foundation for the future, so that they may take hold of that which is life indeed (1 Timothy 6:17-19).

The full experience of our Promised Land is a certainty that awaits every Christian in heaven. But we "may take hold of that which is life indeed" beginning the instant we are saved. Doing so requires a fight! Three enemies conspire to prevent us from experiencing real *life*. **First**, Satan, that serpent of old, will fight us tooth and nail. **Second**, a world filled with evil, suffering, and temptation will entice Christians "to be conceited or to fix their hope on the uncertainty of riches". Or it will try to weigh us down with despair. And **third**, our own flesh will remember the fleeting pleasures of sin and the instant gratification that things of this world offer. Our flesh will lunge for these things. Christians must fight our enemies in order to experience the life that is rightfully ours. We are in a spiritual battle, tantamount to what Israel fought physically.

The Book of Joshua is about Israel's fight for the Promised Land. The battles are intense. Joshua is at the helm, a picture of Jesus as the Commander of God's army. But the man Joshua must not be mistaken for "Yahweh is salvation", so a mysterious figure appears on the scene. Much as Melchizedek appeared in Genesis to reveal that Jesus is the true Priest, the Commander of the Army of the Lord appears in Joshua to reveal that Jesus is the true Commander.

Now it came about when Joshua was by Jericho, that he lifted up his eyes and looked, and behold, a man was standing opposite him with his sword drawn in his hand, and Joshua went to him and said to him, "Are you for us or for our adversaries?" He said, "No; rather I indeed come now as captain of the host of the Lord." And Joshua fell on his face to the earth, and bowed down, and said to him, "what has my Lord to say to his servant?" The captain of the Lord's host said to Joshua, "Remove your sandals from your feet, for the place where you are standing is holy." And Joshua did so (Joshua 5:13-15).

The Captain of the Lord's Army is none other than Jesus Himself. Joshua was required to take off his shoes because Jesus is "Yahweh". Like Moses at the burning bush, Joshua was on holy ground in the presence of I AM WHO I AM. Some may bristle at the proposition that the Lord Jesus is a Warrior, standing in power with sword drawn. Perhaps they have only heard about His sufferings and the meekness of the man who turned the other cheek, even unto His own crucifixion. But enduring Roman scourging, carrying the weight of beams of wood, taking the pain of the nails and the crown of thorns, enduring hours of heaving for breath on the cross, restraining the desire to call for hosts of angels to deliver him alive requires all the attributes of the greatest soldier. The Lord is a Warrior.

And I saw heaven opened, and behold, a white horse, and He who sat on it is called Faithful and True, and in righteousness He judges and wages war. His eyes are a flame of fire, and on his head are many diadems; and He has a name written on Him which no one knows except Himself. He is clothed in a robe dipped in blood, and His name is called the Word of God. And the armies which are in heaven, clothed in fine linen, white and clean, were following Him on white horses. From His mouth comes a sharp sword, so that with it He may strike down the nations, and He will rule them with a rod of iron; and He treads the wine press of the fierce wrath of God, the Almighty. And on His robe and on His thigh He has a name written, "KING OF KINGS, AND LORD OF LORDS" (Revelation 19:11-16).

Jesus came to take away our sin and provide the gift of everlasting life. We are in a battle to take hold of that life. It is our

Promised Land, but we must wage war for it. Like Joshua progressing from city to city, so we must progress in our Christian lives. But we do not go into battle on our own. We are led forth by our Captain. Furthermore, we are invited to fight for His Kingdom, not the other way around. We cannot join His host until we take off our shoes. If we humble ourselves on that holy ground, acknowledging Jesus as our King and Lord, then we join His host. Our sins are instantly forgiven, and we are instantly given eternal life. We enter the battle to take hold of the life that is truly life and to advance the kingdom of God on earth. The Book of Joshua invites us to join the army of the Lord by submitting to the Lord Jesus Christ—the Captain of the Lord's army.

CHAPTER 7

SEEN IN THE DELIVERER

JUDGES

The Book of Judges tells about a series of judges who rule over Israel. But their title can be a bit confusing to the English reader. The Hebrew word for *judge* referred more to a military-style deliverer than to a legal decision maker who sits upon a bench and decides cases. While the deliverer could fulfill a legal function as well, the purpose for which God raised them up in the first place was to bring salvation to the people. In this way, they are like Joshua. They are a picture of the *Captain of the Army of the Lord.*

These judges add something essential to the imagery of the coming Captain. He will be an unlikely and unpredictable Savior. Joshua bowed down to the true Captain (Joshua 5:13-15). Unlike Joshua, the true Captain seemingly came out of nowhere. In contrast to Him, Joshua was groomed by Moses to take over leadership of Israel. Joshua was one of the twelve hand-picked leaders who spied out the Promised Land after the Exodus from Egypt. Upon Israel's fearful withdrawal, Joshua served as Moses' right-hand man as Israel wandered in the desert for forty years. Not only was Joshua the most likely candidate to take over for Moses, he was chosen by God and validated by an astounding miracle. The parting of the Jordan River revealed that he was the unquestioned successor to Moses.

In this, Joshua prefigured Jesus Christ—the Prophet *like* Moses. But for all of his similarities to Jesus, which point forward to Jesus, Joshua was not the Savior of the world. The Book of Judges adds an important wrinkle to the texture with which the books of the Old Testament picture Jesus Christ. Unlike Joshua, the predictable deliverer, God will bring forth *The Deliverer* from among the *unlikely*.

The Book of Judges develops a theme about the *predictability* of sin and the *unpredictability* of salvation. Once in the Promised Land, the behavior of the people is predictable. They will always fall back into sinful practices. Although God created the nation of Israel to be His own special possession, their behavior will mirror the immorality and idolatry of the nations that surround them. Although God provides abundantly for them, their hearts will wander and become unfaithful to Him. This sinfulness becomes predictable as the book of Judges unfolds. No matter how many times God comes through for them, demonstrating His faithfulness to the Covenant, they will break the terms of the contract. Israel's unfaithfulness to God—like ours—is predictable. But from where God's salvation comes is unpredictable.

Each time that Israel strays into apostasy, the Israelites begin to reap what they sow. They experience consequences for their sin, which includes invasion from surrounding nations. As the weight of oppression begins to weigh heavy upon them, they turn back to the God they had forsaken and cry out for deliverance. God in turn raises up a Deliverer (Savior, Captain) from an unlikely place. This cycle of sin, punishment, repentance, and deliverance repeats itself over and over throughout the book. Each time God raises up a Judge, there is this element of unpredictability and unlikelihood. Shortly, we will see why God works this way, but first consider some examples.

The Judges were unlikely Deliverers. When the great Caleb (Joshua's close companion) called for help, God sent Othniel (Judges 1:13), who was the son of Caleb's youngest brother (the least esteemed among the brothers). Among a people who prized right-handedness, God raised up Ehud, who wielded the sword with his left (Judges 3:15). In a patriarchal society, God raises up Deborah from the physically weaker sex (Judges 4:9). Many have heard of Gideon, but forget that he was from the smallest tribe in Israel. His family was obscure (Judges 6:15). When God called him, he was threshing wheat at a secluded winepress. God chose a virtual nobody to save the nation. God chose Tola (Judges 10:1), maybe *because* the name his father gave him means "worm". Jephthah was the son of a prostitute (Judges 11:1). And then there was Samson. Sure, he was physically strong, but readers of the story quickly notice his mental weakness (Judges 16:17). His gullibility and susceptibility to temptation made him an unlikely Deliverer.

When Jesus arrived on the scene from His hometown of

Nazareth, He was greeted by this telling reception: "Nazareth! Can anything good come from there?" (John 1:46). When archeologists uncovered the ruins of Nazareth, they found virtually no coins or items of value. But not only was it small and impoverished, it had a reputation for debauchery. Of all the places in Israel where Jesus might have grown up, God's design placed Him in Nazareth. And He didn't grow up in the Temple Courts being groomed for the ministry by the religious elite. He didn't wear flowing religious robes or attach Scripture boxes to His forehead. He didn't pray on the street corners of Jerusalem to be admired by the people of Jerusalem.

Rather, He grew up the son of a carpenter. He was raised as a common tradesman. The only thing that would mark this carpenter from Nazareth to be the Deliverer of Israel and the Savior of the world is that God revealed His plan to take the base things of this world to shame the important.

But God has chosen the foolish things of the world to shame the wise, and God has chosen the weak things of the world to shame the things which are strong, and the base things of the world and the despised God has chosen, the things that are not, so that He may nullify the things that are, so that no man may boast before God (1 Corinthians 1:27-29).

The Book of Judges presents a series of deliverers that have in common their own *unlikelihood.* In so doing, the power that they exhibit is shown to be from God. Deliverance is therefore not a result of man's greatness, and the glory doesn't go to man. God reduced the size of Gideon's army from thousands upon thousands to only a few hundred. So when they won, everyone knew that the battle belonged to the Lord. In the same way, the message of Jesus also looks like foolishness to natural human reasoning.

The Gospel claims that a humble carpenter from Nazareth is also the Almighty Creator of heaven and earth. The Gospel claims that God is One, but at the same time, He is three. The Gospel claims that a man reduced to the shame of dying naked upon a cross is God's plan to save the world. The Gospel claims that a man crucified and buried for three days conquered the grave and walked out. The Gospel claims that all human effort to be righteous amounts to vanity and our only hope for salvation is simple faith in Someone we have never seen, heard, smelled, tasted, or touched. The Gospel makes no appeal to our physical senses, nor does it cater to our human reasoning. Yet it commands us to believe.

For the word of the cross is foolishness to those who are perishing, but to us who are being saved it is the power of God. For it is written, "I will destroy the wisdom of the wise, and the cleverness of the clever I will set aside." Where is the wise man? Where is the scribe? Where is the debater of this age? Has not God made foolish the wisdom of the world? For since in the wisdom of God the world through its wisdom did not come to know God, God was well-pleased through the foolishness of the message preached to save those who believe. For indeed Jews ask for signs and Greeks search for wisdom; but we preach Christ crucified, to Jews a stumbling block and to Gentiles foolishness, but to those who are the called, both Jews and Greeks, Christ the power of God and the wisdom of God. Because the foolishness of God is wiser than men, and the weakness of God is stronger than men (1 Corinthians 1:18-25).

Israel's failings in the Book of Judges are indicative of the human condition. We have all been caught in cycles of sin because sin is a part of our nature. Like Israel, we are influenced by the world around us and increasingly participate in the world's sins. There is a fleeting pleasure that comes with sin, but before long we begin to reap what we sow. Consequences overtake us, and sin becomes a heavy taskmaster. If we will only cry out to God, "I am helpless. Save me!", then there is a Savior who stands ready to deliver us. He is not like the Judges of Israel who could only provide temporary deliverance.

After being delivered, Israel would always cycle back into sin and punishment. Even today, people struggle with cycles of sin. They may overcome an addiction for a time, but soon they will fall back into it again. But our Judge is able to save and deliver. He can erase the death penalty that we are owed, but He can also break the power of sin that previously was unbreakable. Jesus Christ came to set sinners free from sin. He alone is able to break the cycle!

Therefore He is able also to save forever those who draw near to God through Him (Hebrews 7:25).

Salvation comes from an unlikely place—Nazareth. The Savior is unpredictably ordinary—a carpenter. His message is foolishly simple and pays no heed to the religious pretenses of men—"Believe in the Lord Jesus Christ and you will be saved" (Acts 16:31). The message offends those who are wise in their own eyes, but it is the power of God to save those who realize their need to be saved from the penalty and power of sin.

CHAPTER 8

SEEN IN THE REDEEMER

RUTH

The books about Israel taking possession of the Promised Land (Joshua and Judges) are filled with violence and bloodshed. From the shadows of this darkness, an image emerges of a coming Captain of the Lord's Army. He is to be feared. With robe dipped in blood and sword drawn, He will conquer the enemies of God. And for this, we should be glad. It means that every man who presses children into the slave trade will be judged. Every Adolf Hitler, every Joseph Stalin, every abusive husband and every mother who abandons her children will be recompensed. A world that sometimes feels intolerably unjust will experience absolute justice for the first time since the Garden of Eden.

But unless there is a provision for sinners like us to be shown mercy, we could not celebrate the judgment of God because we also would face condemnation. In our desperate state, the blood of the Lamb placed upon the wood of the cross becomes our great victory and our reason to have hope in the coming of the victorious Captain of the Lord's army. After all of the bloodshed we find in Joshua and Judges, the reader needs a respite. We need to come up for air. We need to catch our breath and remember what drove our Deliverer into battle in the first place—His love for us.

Providing much needed balance to the picture of a Warrior emerging from a gruesome battle, the book of Ruth pictures Jesus as a Groom pursuing His Bride in a beautiful love story. Consistent with the theme of sin's devastating effects, Ruth suffers the death of her first husband. Her sister and her mother-in-law also experience the same. So the three women are left alone, and that in a hostile land where single women have little protection. Naomi, the mother-in-law, is an alien in the land of Moab, but her two daughters-in-law are natives there.

Having nothing, Naomi chooses to return to Israel—her homeland—and counsels her daughters to stay in theirs. Her life a mess, Orpah agrees to part ways with her mother-in-law. But in a beautiful display of loyalty, Ruth says to Naomi, "Do not urge me to leave you or turn back from following you, for where you go, I will go, and where you lodge, I will lodge. Your people shall be my people, and your God, my God. Where you die, I will die, and there I will be buried. Thus may the Lord do to me, and worse, if anything but death parts you and me" (Ruth 1:16-17).

Significantly, Ruth places her trust in Yahweh rather than the gods of the Moabites. As she enters Israel with her mother-in-law, she is completely dependent upon this God in whom she has placed her trust. What will she find there? She has no land, no dowry, no wealth, and probably not much more than the clothes on her back. She has no protector. How will the followers of Yahweh treat her?

Upon arriving, Naomi and Ruth stumble upon an Israelite who was related to Naomi's deceased husband. Boaz is his name, and he is a man of great wealth. Boaz pursues her, redeems Ruth's devastated life, loves her with the passion of the most self-sacrificing husband, and in so doing, paints a picture of Jesus Christ. Like Ruth, each of us has been ravaged by the curse of sin. But like Boaz, Jesus waits for us to come to Him, and He is ready to redeem our lives from the pit. The love story between a husband and wife is developed in the New Testament. It is not a picture of Jesus and an individual believer. Rather it is the picture of Jesus redeeming that whole body of humanity that places trust in Him. The Book of Ruth gives a picture of the love of Jesus for the Church. Christ Jesus loves and cares for His people.

Husbands, love your wives, just as Christ also loved the church and gave Himself up for her, so that He might sanctify her, having cleansed her by the washing of water with the word (Ephesians 5:25-26).

The Book of Ruth is a beautiful love story. It tells of a man and his bride, but it points to the greatest love of all. "Greater love has no one than this, that one lay down his life for his friends" (John 15:13). But in case someone were to doubt that the story of Boaz and Ruth really has this deeper layer of meaning, in case someone has trouble accepting that Jesus loves him or her with so great a love, God imbedded one more clue in the closing verses of the book.

Boaz took Ruth, and she became his wife . . . and she gave birth to a son... Then she said to Naomi, "Blessed is the Lord who has not left you without a redeemer today, and may his name become famous in Israel. May He also be to you a restorer of life and a sustainer of your old age." . . . Then Naomi took the child and laid him in her lap, and became his nurse (Ruth 4:13-16).

God's love had not overlooked this poor woman in her old age. Imagine how Ruth's child energized Naomi's life throughout the remainder of her life. What a sense of hope and of purpose was restored to her as she helped to raise this child, whose name was Obed. The love of God would never forget or forsake anyone who flees to Him. Naomi fled to find refuge under the wings of Yahweh—the God of Israel—and He welcomed her with His Kinsman Redeemer.

And what of this child? "He is the father of Jesse, the father of David" (Ruth 4:17). Obed grew to become a man, and later, the grandfather of the one God chose to be king of Israel. The significance of this clue must not be missed. Boaz, Obed, Jesse, and David are in the family line of Jesus! Now we can see why the Scriptures made note of the fact that "Boaz came from Bethlehem" (Ruth 2:4). A son of Boaz, descended from him, born in that little town of Bethlehem, would be just like his father. He would redeem a bride for Himself, give Himself to her, and love her forever. The descendant of Boaz is our Redeemer. His name—Jesus—is famous in Israel and to the ends of the earth. He is the Restorer of Life to those devastated by the curse of sin and death. Blessed is the Lord who has not left us without a Redeemer today!

CHAPTER 9

SEEN IN THE REJECTED KING
FIRST SAMUEL

The Book of First Samuel picks up where Judges left off. The Book of Ruth was a kind of parenthesis, capturing a picture of God's love displayed through certain individuals during the time of the Judges. But First Samuel continues the overall narrative of the Bible. It brings the story to a point of transition whereby Israel's first King (Saul) replaces her last Judge (Samuel) and the Theocracy becomes a Monarchy. Consistent with the cycles found in Judges (apostasy, punishment, repentance, deliverance), the Book of First Samuel picks up when Israel is at her worst, the bottom of the cycle. The sons of Eli are supposed to be priests that bring Israel to God, but even they are participating in the worst forms of immorality. Due to the spiritual condition of Israel, God has removed His hand of protection, and the Philistines are attacking.

As the story unfolds, representations of Jesus Christ emerge. The ineffectiveness of the Ark of the Covenant to rescue Israel reveals our need for a greater Ark (1 Samuel 4). Samuel arises as the last Judge. He is a great prophet and priest, but Israel's demand for a human *king* and the subsequent failure of Saul reveals that God alone is fit to be King. Jesus is the Ark of our rescue. He is the Prophet-Priest-King that God promised. He is God in human flesh.

Torah (the first five books of the Bible) clearly revealed that Messiah would fulfill the role of Prophet, Priest, and King. As to His prophetic office, He would be like Moses, only greater (Deuteronomy 18:15-18, 34:10-12). As to His priesthood, He would be like Melchizedek and therefore greater than all the Levites (Genesis 14:18-20). As to His Kingdom, it is everlasting, for "the scepter shall not depart from Judah" (Genesis 49:10), and Jesus is the Final King among all who descended from Judah's line. Each of these offices (prophet, priest, king) receive thousands of layers of added meaning, much of which we have seen. Samuel brings two of these offices together and in significant ways points to Jesus as the One who will ultimately fulfill all three. Israel's rejection of God as their King foreshadows their rejection of Jesus.

Samuel was born and grew up in an unusual way. His mother Hannah was barren but had approached God in the Holy Tabernacle. When Samuel was born, she dedicated him to the Lord and burst into joyful celebration, recording a song that prefigures the song that Mary would sing. Hannah's praise—the prayer of a godly mother—came by the inspiration of the same Holy Spirit who led Mary to offer hers. Compare 1 Samuel 2 with Luke 1:46-55 to see how the hearts of these two mothers exalted the Lord. Samuel was born despite Hannah's long-time barrenness, and Jesus was born despite Mary's virginity.

At the age of twelve, Jesus tarried in the Temple for a day while his parents returned home (Luke 2:41-52). Samuel was left to grow up in the House of God training to become a Priest. But those who were outwardly trained to be priests did not necessarily have a true relationship with Almighty God. And this was the case with the natural sons of the priest (Eli) under whom Samuel was in training. As they committed debauchery, even in the midst of their religious ritual, God began to speak to Samuel and added to this young Priest the office of Prophet.

Now the boy Samuel was ministering to the Lord before Eli. And word from the Lord was rare in those days, visions were infrequent . . . the lamp of God had not yet gone out, and Samuel was lying down in the temple of the Lord where the ark of God was, that the Lord called Samuel; and he said, "Here I am" (1 Samuel 3:1-4).

From this time forward, Samuel hears the voice of the Lord and speaks for Him as a Prophet. Israel at times receives the Prophet, just like they welcomed Jesus when He gave them bread, performed miracles, and entered Jerusalem triumphantly. But when Samuel told them what they didn't want to hear, they turned against him. Ultimately, the people rejected Samuel as their ruler, just as they would later reject Jesus with shouts of "Crucify! Crucify!".

Significantly, the turning point upon which the will of the people hinged was their desire to have a king. When Jesus entered Jerusalem, the people wanted Him to set up His Kingdom and overthrow

Rome. A week later, when they saw Him beaten and bloody at the hands of the Roman king's soldiers, they were ready to do away with Him. Israel always wanted an earthly king like that of the nations around them. They wanted a king to make Israel great. But in this desire, they rejected God as their Theocratic Ruler. Upon his rejection, Samuel receives comforting words from God that once again point us to Jesus the Anointed King.

But the thing was displeasing in the sight of Samuel when they said, "Give us a king to judge us." And Samuel prayed to the Lord. The Lord said to Samuel, "Listen to the voice of the people in regard to all that they say to you, for they have not rejected you, but they have rejected Me from being king over them" (1 Samuel 8:6-7).

Jesus alone is fit to be King of Israel because He alone is both God and man. When He returns to sit upon the throne, His Kingdom will not be a monarchy. It will be a Theocracy, because the King is God. What Samuel prefigured, he also fell short of. He was a prophet and a priest and a very important figure since he combined both, but Jesus is *the* Prophet-Priest-King, the Savior of the world, the God who was there in the beginning and will be there in the end—the I AM.

The king that Israel picked when they rejected God turned out to be an *anti-type* or *countertype.* If Samuel was a type of Christ, then Saul was an anti-Christ. God had warned Israel.

This will be the procedure of the king who will reign over you: he will take your sons and place them for himself in his chariots and among his horsemen and they will run before his chariots. He will also take your daughters for perfumers and cooks and bakers. He will take the best of your fields and your vineyards and your olive groves and give them to his servants (1 Samuel 8:11-14).

Saul proved to be this kind of self-serving king. Not only so, but as things began to unravel for him, he descended into the worst forms of idolatry. He started fairly well. The people esteemed him because he stood head and shoulders above the people of Israel. He even won some victories when he obeyed the counsel of Samuel. But by the end of his life, he was consulting with a witch (1 Samuel 28:7). Rather than representing Yahweh, he spiraled out of control and became a representative of Satan, one of the first antichrist figures in the Bible. Compare him with the genuine Christ and how He functioned as the true King.

For even the Son of Man did not come to be served, but to serve, and to give His life a ransom for many (Mark 10:45).

Like Samuel, Jesus was rejected as Israel's Ruler. On the day of Jesus' rejection, the people shouted that Barabbas be given to them instead. "They shouted back, 'No, not him! Give us Barabbas!' Now Barabbas had taken part in an uprising" (John 18:40).

The name Barabbas literally means "son of the father". But the "son of the father" that Israel wanted was an imposter—a common criminal with a wicked heart. He was like Saul, a pretender to the throne, and anti-type of the Christ. Meanwhile, the genuine Son of God and King of Kings stood right before them. Jesus was so different from earthly kings, having come to serve rather than to be served, that the people didn't recognize Him. He came to give His life as a ransom (a payment to buy back their very lives), but all they wanted was the passing benefits of living in a dominant kingdom of this world.

Repeating the mistake they made in the days of Samuel, where they chose a counterfeit over God Himself, Israel chose Barabbas over the God of the Universe standing before them in human flesh. After Jesus triumphed over death by rising from the dead, Peter explained to all of Jerusalem the folly of what they had done, and with these words, he also calls us to receive Jesus as the Lord of our lives:

The God of Abraham, Isaac and Jacob, the God of our fathers, has glorified his servant Jesus, the one whom you delivered and disowned in the presence of Pilate, when he had decided to release Him. But you disowned the Holy and Righteous One and asked for a murderer to be granted to you, but put to death the Prince of life, the one whom God raised from the dead, a fact to which we are witnesses (Acts 3:13-15).

Jesus is the Prophet-Priest-King. He is God in the flesh. But preferring to be like the nations around them, Israel chose a common sinful man instead of Him. Just as they did when they rejected God and took Saul as king, they rejected Jesus and took Barabbas. And now the same question comes to each of us: Who will we accept as King of our lives? Will we place ourselves, as ordinary and sinful as we are, in that position? Will we reject Jesus? Or will we recognize Him for the King that He is?

CHAPTER 10

SEEN IN THE DAVIDIC KING
SECOND SAMUEL

The two Samuels are really just volumes of the same book. The second continues the narrative of the history of Israel. It also continues the themes of First Samuel. God raised up a Judge—Samuel—to deliver Israel. As a great *type* of Christ, he brought together the offices of Prophet and Priest. Samuel was both. His abnormal birth and childhood devotion to studying in the Temple also foreshadow Jesus. But Samuel was not fit to be King. God alone is able to fill that office. When the people of Israel reject God as their King, shouts of *"No, not Him! Give us Barabbas!"* should echo in the reader's mind. Israel gets Saul as their king in place of God, just as they will later choose Barabbas over *God in the flesh.*

As the story of Israel's history continues to unfold, God acquiesces to Israel's demand for a King, and mercifully, after Israel's choice of Saul proves to be a great failure, God provides a great King. David—God's choice—completes the profile of the coming

Prophet-Priest-King that the Books of Samuel anticipate. David is a prophet and a king, but not a priest. Many of his words as a prophet are recorded for us in the vast Book of Psalms, which we will study when we come to it. His Psalm 22 is perhaps the most astounding prophecy of Jesus anywhere in the Bible. But in 2 Samuel, David's office as *King* is crucial for our understanding of Jesus as King.

Your house and your kingdom shall endure before Me forever; your throne shall be established forever (2 Samuel 7:16).

The importance of this—the Davidic Covenant—is hard to overstate. With these words and many others in the context of 2 Samuel 7, David receives the promise that he will always have a descendant to sit on the throne. As history unfolds, David's sons arise in succession to take the throne. Solomon receives it from David. Rehoboam receives it from Solomon. After them is a long succession of Davidic Kings.

At a certain point, the promise appears to be in peril. Invading superpowers will eventually overrun the Kingdom, and it will appear that the Davidic Covenant has failed. But God returns His people to the land, and even though imposters like Herod assume the throne, the scepter truly belongs to a son of David. This is why Jesus' birth in Bethlehem—the City of David—to Mary and (as it was supposed) to Joseph is so significant. Both Mary and Joseph descend from David's line of kings. God has preserved the genealogical records of both Joseph and Mary for us. They are found in Matthew 1 and Luke 3 and, amazingly, both descend from the line of Kings that began with David.

What's more, this covenant is "established forever", which means it will continue for all eternity. How could the prophet Nathan, who spoke these words to David, make such a certain claim about eternity—with all of its infinite possibilities? God inspired the prophecy, knowing that the scepter would pass from son of David to son of David but finally arrive in the hand of a son of David who is also the eternal Son of God. It would be like runners passing a baton, but when the baton comes to a final runner, He runs forever. Jesus has taken the scepter, and he will never relinquish it. This son of David is the eternal King!

Recalling how promises about *the scepter* trace all the way back to the Garden of Eden will solidify our understanding of how significant the Davidic Covenant really is. Adam was commissioned to rule over creation as God's representative. Because sin infected the human race, the scepter was surrendered. Satan became a ruler over this world. But God chose a man—Abraham—and made a nation out of him. Isaac (not Ishmael) would carry on the Promise of a coming "Seed" to rule the world. Jacob (not Esau) would receive the promise from his father Isaac. Among the twelve sons of Jacob, Judah received the all-important promise.

The scepter shall not depart from Judah, nor the ruler's staff from between his feet, until Shiloh comes, and to him shall be the obedience of the peoples (Genesis 49:10).

The Davidic Covenant picks up the promise where it was left off—belonging to someone from the Tribe of Judah. David was only an insignificant shepherd boy belonging to the Tribe of Judah. When

God chose David, He continued revealing the family tree of the coming King of the world.

Now therefore, thus you shall say to My servant David, "Thus says the Lord of hosts, 'I took you from the pasture, from following the sheep, to be ruler over My people Israel'" (2 Samuel 7:8).

Recall that Biblical Prophecy continually narrows the field of interpretation, centering in upon one promised Messiah. Pretend prophecies are vague and are unlimited in the field of interpretation. Any event in human history could be construed to fit whatever it is that men like Nostradamus said. But the Bible is a coherent story. And more than a story, the historical references that we find in the Bible actually comport to what archeologists and historians observe. David was a real king. The Temple his son Solomon built was one of the seven wonders of the ancient world. The western wall of it stands to this day. One can visit Bethlehem and see the City of David for himself.

Within the narrative of actual history, God spoke through prophets and continually zeroed us in upon the coming King. Ordinary men have no control over their ancestry. If Jesus was an imposter and was deliberately trying to make Himself fit the prophecies of the King, then how did He control his ancestry? The entire country of Israel was only a speck compared to the vast lands of earth. Her population was never very significant. And then, Judah was only one of twelve tribes. And within that one Tribe, the line of kings descended from David narrowed the field to a still smaller group with the potential to be king. But God knew His eternal Son, so for our sake, He pinpointed from whom the King would come. The prophet Nathan foretold that Messiah had to be a son of David, and Jesus was.

CHAPTER 11

SEEN IN THE KING OF PEACE
FIRST KINGS

The reign of the son of David ushered in an unprecedented period of peace and prosperity for the nation of Israel. Solomon was the first descendant of David to sit upon the throne. His name derives from the Hebrew word for *peace*, "shalom". Second Samuel revealed the covenant that God made with David and his descendants forever. One of his sons would be King forever. Solomon was the first to follow David, and his Kingdom was a picture of the blessing that the Son of David will bring. First Kings reveals what the reign of Jesus Christ will mean for Israel and the nations. Jesus Christ will bring "Glory to God in the highest, and on earth peace among men with whom He is pleased" (Luke 2:14).

He had peace on all sides around about him. So Judah and Israel lived in safety, every man under his vine and his fig tree, from Dan even to Beersheba, all the days of Solomon (1 Kings 4:24-25).

Solomon, the King of Peace, had peace on all sides. He had

good relationships with the kings of the surrounding nations. In fact, they saw the blessing of Yahweh upon the nation of Israel and blessed Yahweh on account of the great favor He showed to His people. They had wealth and provision for all. Even nature itself seemed to favor Israel. It gave rain in season and abundance of crops. There were no needy people among the Israelites because those who had extra would allow the poor to glean from the edges of their fields and from that which fell to the ground. There were no plagues. Wild animals that can harm people were kept at bay. There was no rising superpower to threaten Israel because Israel was the greatest nation on earth. They were fulfilling the purpose for which God called Abraham, Isaac, and Jacob and made a chosen nation. They were blessed, in order to be a blessing.

The nations of earth were drawn to Israel. The Queen of an African nation came to visit Solomon because the light of Israel was spreading far and wide. Her words to Solomon demonstrate not only how blessed Israel was but also how the peace of Israel was a magnet that drew the nations to believe in the God of Israel.

It was a true report which I heard in my own land about your words and wisdom. Nevertheless I did not believe the reports, until I came and my eyes had seen it. And behold, the half was not told to me. You exceed in wisdom and prosperity the report which I heard. How blessed are your men, how blessed are these your servants who stand before you continually and hear your wisdom. Blessed be the Lord your God who delighted in you to set you on the throne of Israel; because the Lord loved Israel forever, therefore He made you king, to do justice and righteousness (1 Kings 10:6-9).

Solomon provided a glimpse of the Kingdom of Peace. He brought peace to Israel "so that all the peoples of the earth may know that the Lord is God; there is no one else" (1 Kings 8:60). Unfortunately, since Solomon was a man infected by sin like the rest of us, the period of peace and prosperity was short lived. Solomon fell into many temptations and turned away from the God of Israel. When he did, the Lighthouse to the nations began to shine only a dim beacon to the nations. Israel needed a righteous king to sit upon the throne. Here again, the story cries out for Jesus. He alone is righteous. He is the only sinless person who has ever lived. He alone can bring a lasting Kingdom of Peace. Solomon was a type of Christ, but Christ is the King of Peace. At His first appearing, He brought peace between God and man.

Therefore, having been justified by faith, we have peace with God through our Lord Jesus Christ (Romans 5:1).

At His second coming, Jesus Christ will sit on David's throne and reign in the City of Jerusalem. The nations will be gathered to Him. From Jerusalem, He will reign over a Kingdom of Peace that will last 1000 years. At the end of that time, Satan will be allowed one last stand. He will tempt people to join his rebellion, and many will. But that rebellion will soon be crushed, at which time Christ will set up an eternal Kingdom of Peace. In this eternal state, known as heaven, there will be no more pain, no more tears. The King of Peace will receive glory, and His subjects will receive peace and prosperity.

Then I saw a new heaven and a new earth; for the first heaven and the first earth passed away, and there is no longer any sea. And I saw the holy city, new

Jerusalem, coming down out of heaven from God, made ready as a bride adorned for her husband. And I heard a loud voice from the throne, saying, "Behold, the tabernacle of God is among men, and He will dwell among men, and they shall be His people, and God Himself will be among them, and He will wipe away every tear from their eyes; and there will no longer be any death; there will no longer be any mourning, or crying, or pain; the first things have passed away" (Revelation 21:1-4).

What makes heaven so eternally wonderful is the presence of God in our midst. And this is what Solomon's Temple symbolized. David had it in his heart to build a Temple for God. Solomon was the one to carry out that vision. Having finished the amazing structure, Solomon dedicated it to the Lord. At that very moment, a cloud filled the place. It was a manifestation of the glory of the Lord. All the people were utterly overwhelmed, captured by joy and a sense of absolute awe. The Temple had become a special dwelling place for Almighty God.

When Jesus came to earth, just a baby lying in the manger, most of Israel was totally unaware that God was in their midst. The Temple was a wonder of the ancient world, but its purpose was to point the world to Jesus Christ. The Temple meant that God would come and dwell among men.

And the Word became flesh, and dwelt among us, and we saw His glory, glory as of the only begotten from the Father, full of grace and truth (John 1:14).

Jesus is called "the Word" partly because the Scriptures—God's Word—speak of Him so much. The chief purpose of the Bible is to reveal Jesus Christ. God gave His Word in order that we would know

His Son. But John 1:14 not only calls Jesus "the Word", it tells us that He came in person to Planet Earth. John said elsewhere, "What was from the beginning, what we have heard, what we have seen with our eyes, what we have looked at and touched with our hands, concerning the Word of Life" (1 John 1:1). The Son of God took on flesh and walked among men. The world was made through Him, and yet here He was in flesh and blood—the presence of God among men. Jesus Himself told us that the Temple pointed to Him.

The Jews then said to Him, "What sign do you show us as your authority for doing these things?" Jesus answered them, "Destroy this temple, and in three days I will raise it up." The Jews then said, "It took forty-six years to build this temple, and will you raise it up in three days?" But He was speaking of the temple of His body. So when He was raised from the dead, His disciples remembered that He said this; and they believed the Scripture and the word which Jesus had spoken (John 2:18-22).

Do you believe the Scripture and the word that Jesus spoke? Do you believe that He rose from the dead on the third day? The Temple was destroyed shortly after Jesus died, and it has yet to be rebuilt. But the testimony of John is that he heard, saw, and touched Jesus Christ after He rose from the dead. More than five hundred people bore witness to the same experience in the weeks following the resurrection. Thomas wasn't there the first time, so he said, "unless I see in His hands the imprint of the nails, and put my finger into the place of the nails, and put my hand into His side, I will not believe" (John 20:25).

Eight days later, Jesus appeared to Thomas and said, "Peace be with you" (20:26). He offered to let Thomas touch His hands and side, saying "Reach here with your finger, and see My hands, and reach here your hand and put it into My side; and do not be unbelieving, but believing" (20:27). "Thomas answered and said to Him, 'My Lord and my God!' Jesus said to him, 'Because you have seen Me, have you believed? Blessed are they who do not see, and yet believe.'" (20:28-29)

How about you? Is the Word of God enough for you to believe? Even now, Jesus speaks, "Peace be with you". Will you remember how Solomon typified the King of Peace and how the Temple also typified God dwelling among men? Will you take God, not blindly, but at His Word? Will you believe in Jesus?

CHAPTER 12

SEEN IN THE MIRACLE WORKER
SECOND KINGS

The Book of 2 Kings opens with a story that establishes a theme that will run throughout. The kings of Israel have become exceedingly wicked and have utterly forsaken Yahweh. Ahaziah takes a fall and inquires of a false god as to whether or not he will recover. To this evil king and those who follow him, God sends prophets to rebuke them. For example, Elijah says to Ahaziah, "Is it because there is no God in Israel that you are going to inquire of Baal-zebub, the god of Ekron? Now therefore thus says the Lord, 'You shall not come down from the bed where you have gone up, but you shall surely die'"(2 Kings 1:3-4).

Meanwhile, as wicked kings reign in the north of Israel, the kingdom is divided and Davidic kings reign in the south. Some of them are God-fearing. Others are just like the kings of the north. But even the "good" ones are prone to compromising with evil. Taken together, the kings represent the human condition. We are dead in our sins. But God does not abandon His people. Instead, He sends them prophets. These are the representatives of God and types of

Jesus Christ in the book of 2 Kings.

Elijah was the most prominent prophet in First Kings. He is succeeded by Elisha in Second Kings. They lack the political power of the kings, but God gives them power from heaven to supersede the corrupted power of those who are in positions of authority. As the kings of Israel went, to large measure, so went the people of Israel. The wicked King Ahab was a worshipper of Baal, so Baal worship had infected the land. Elijah was sent by God to oppose this evil, and it all came to a head on Mount Carmel. God literally sent fire down from heaven to demonstrate that Elijah's God—Yahweh—was the true God. Witnessing that miracle, the people experienced a great revival. They turned back in mass to Yahweh and destroyed altars to Baal. Elijah's successor performed even more miracles. Elijah and Elisha point forward to the miracle worker of the New Testament—Jesus Christ.

During the time of Elisha, there was famine in the land of Israel because of disobedience to the Covenant. Creditors were threatening to take a poor widow's sons as slaves if she didn't quickly satisfy a debt she owed. But she was at the end of her rope. She had nothing to give and no way to make money.

Elisha said to her, "what shall I do for you? Tell me, what do you have in the house?" And she said, "Your maidservant has nothing in the house except a jar of oil." Then he said, "Go, borrow vessels at large for yourself from all your neighbors, even empty vessels; do not get a few. And you shall go in and shut the door behind you and your sons, and pour out into all the vessels, and you shall set aside what is full." So she went from him and shut the door behind her and her sons; they were bringing the vessels to her and she poured. When the vessels were full, she said to her son, "Bring me another vessel." And he said to her, "There is not one vessel more." And the oil stopped (2 Kings 4:2-6).

On another occasion, a woman from Shunem, who used to feed Elisha when he passed through town, suffered a tragedy. Her son went out to work with his father in the fields. He got a bad headache and so returned home as the father continued in the field. The boy sat in his mother's lap, trying to recover. But he only got worse. Before the father even returned from work, the boy died. Leaving the dead boy in the guest room that the family often provided for Elisha, the mother ran past the father in the field, yelled to him as she passed, and went on to look for Elisha. The woman understood that her husband, who was an ordinary man, could do no good for their son in this situation. She needed a miracle worker.

When Elisha came into the house, behold the lad was dead and laid on his bed. So he entered and shut the door behind them both and prayed to the Lord. And he went up and lay on the child, and put his mouth on his mouth and his eyes on his eyes and his hands on his hands, and he stretched himself on him; and the flesh of the child became warm. Then he returned and walked in the house once back and forth, and went up and stretched himself on him; and the lad sneezed seven times and the lad opened his eyes. He called Gehazi and said, "Call this Shunammite." So he called her. And when she came in to him, he said, "Take up your son." Then she went in and fell at his feet and bowed herself to the ground, and she took up her son and went out (2 Kings 4:32-37).

Elijah and Elisha had no power of their own to effect miracles. Rather, they prayed to the Lord, and He was pleased to work miracles through them. On one occasion, Elisha told a foreigner named Naaman to go and dip himself in the Jordan River seven times. Our word "baptize" literally means "to dip" or "plunge". John the Baptist baptized Israelites (including Jesus) in the Jordan River. When Naaman dipped, he was healed of leprosy. But John the Baptist (who was a prophet like Elijah and Elisha) told about a coming Prophet who was also more than a prophet.

And he was preaching , and saying, "After me One is coming who is mightier than I, and I am not fit to stoop down and untie the thong of His sandals. I baptized you with water; but He will baptize you with the Holy Spirit" (John 1:7-8).

Jesus is the One whom the miracle-working prophets reveal. Jesus was a miracle worker who effected miracles by the power He had within Himself. Being God, He could not only heal a physical body of leprosy but He could change the spiritual state of the person. Jesus can heal the heart and clean the soul. The miracles of Elijah and Elisha pointed to Him. Jesus was the one who truly provided for a desperate widow who had nothing left but a jar of oil. Similarly, when at the wedding of Cana another woman—Jesus' own mother Mary—shared with Him the social catastrophe of their hosts running out of wine (John 2:1-11), Jesus gave orders to go get jars. He was ready to reveal His miracle-working power.

Likewise as with the Shunammite whose son was raised back to life, Jesus saw a woman grieving over the casket of her dead son.

When the Lord saw her, He felt compassion for her, and said to her, "Do not weep." And He came up and touched the coffin; and the bearers came to a halt. And He said, "Young man, I say to you, arise!" The dead man sat up and began to speak. And Jesus gave him back to his mother (Luke 7:13-15).

The parallels with the Elisha story are striking, but also notice the differences. Notice the reaction of the crowd. "Fear gripped them all, and they began glorifying God, saying, 'A great prophet has arisen among us!' and, 'God has visited His people'" (Luke 7:16). Elisha had to stretch out upon the boy and continue in faith as little by little life was restored to the body. Jesus, on the other hand, spoke a word, and the man was instantly and completely healed. Jesus had the power to heal within Himself. The people were right to say that a prophet was among them. Surely they remembered the Elisha story, and many of them would have made the connection.

The miracle validated Jesus as a prophet. But the crowd probably didn't realize the extent of what they were saying when they said, "*God* has visited His people". They spoke prophetically, because although they didn't grasp it at the time, what they said was *literally* true. God in the flesh stood among them, and He demonstrated His absolute power over nature, over death, over all things by raising someone from the dead with a spoken command. The miracles of Elijah and Elisha call us to repent of our wickedness, because we are like the kings of Israel. We are like the wandering sheep of Israel. But God sent a Prophet, yes, God Himself visited His people, and He is our only hope of being physically and spiritually healed.

CHAPTER 13

SEEN IN THE ARK OF THE COVENANT

FIRST CHRONICLES

God provided extensive historical records about the genealogy of the tribes of Israel. For this we should be exceedingly thankful, because it provides evidence for believing in Jesus, since His family tree is recorded, and prophets foretold from what family tree the Promised King would descend. First Chronicles provides evidence that the Scepter belongs to Jesus. But the lists can make for some difficult reading, and too many people never make it to the midpoint of the book where it returns to stories and the *Ark of the Covenant* takes center stage. The Ark of the Covenant is very prominent in the Old Testament, and it clearly points to Jesus Christ.

There is a lot of interest in finding the lost Ark of the Covenant. Indiana Jones looked for it, and network TV would have us believe that searching for it is a worthy pursuit. But the actual structure was never what truly mattered. Rather, we would do well to search for its meaning, to make its meaning our treasure, and to find the One whom the Ark was given to reveal. The Ark means salvation.

The Ark was only a wooden box made of acacia wood and overlaid with gold. It had rings on the sides so that poles could be inserted and the ark could be transported without being touched. Inside the Ark were three things that reminded the Israelites of their sinfulness.

First, there were the Ten Commandments written in stone. It was not the first set because those were broken before Moses could even make it down the mountain. The second set, again written in stone, reminded Israel of their law breaking.

Second, there was Aaron's staff that had budded. When Israel rebelled against Moses and Aaron, essentially asking "what makes you so special?", God squashed the rebellion by telling Aaron to hold out his staff. New shoots burst out from that dry stick to force the people to acknowledge whom it was that God had chosen.

Third, there was a jar of manna. Manna represented God's provision, but God gave it in response to the people's grumbling. Even once they had it, they complained about its lack of taste. So, the Ark contained three constant reminders of Israel's sin, failure, and deep need for salvation. God had given them a Covenant, but the Ark of the Covenant reminded them that they didn't have within themselves the necessary righteousness to keep it.

But thanks be to God for His salvation, for atop the Ark was the Mercy Seat. It was gold, but what was put upon it represented Israel's cleansing from the sin inside of them. The High Priest would sprinkle blood upon the Mercy Seat. On each side of the Mercy Seat, there were cherubs made of hammered gold. The presence of God remained in a special way above the Mercy Seat between the cherubim. This pictured what is true in heaven. God is surrounded by angels who worship Him continually, and sinful people can only approach Him by His mercy. But sinful people easily forget how *holy* God really is, so 1 Chronicles 13 is a crucial story for us to hear.

David and all Israel went up to Baalah, that is, to Kiriath-jearim, which belongs to Judah, to bring up from there the ark of God, the Lord who is enthroned above the cherubim, where His name is called. They carried the ark of God on a new cart . . . David and all Israel were celebrating before God with all their might, even with songs and with lyres, harps, tambourines, cymbals, and with trumpets. When they came to the threshing floor of Chidon, Uzza put out his hand to hold the ark, because the oxen nearly upset it. The anger of the Lord burned against Uzza, so He struck him down because he put out his hand to the ark; and he died there before God (1 Chronicles 13:6-10).

David was deeply troubled by God's judgment upon Uzza. It took David quite some time before he was able to come to terms with it. And so it is with us when God allows someone we love to die. We have trouble accepting that God alone has an absolute right to number the days of the people he creates. But as hard as it is for us to hear, we need to know that God is holy. Every day that we spend walking above the dust of the earth, rather than returning to it (for dust we are and to dust we shall return), is a gift of His mercy.

"David was afraid of God that day, saying, 'How can I bring the Ark of God home to me?' So David did not take the Ark with him to the City of David" (1 Chronicles 13:12-13). But later David came to embrace both the holiness and the love of God. The Ark of the Covenant and the God it symbolized became the burning passion of David's life. His life ambition changed, and what he wanted most was to build a Temple in Jerusalem to house the Ark of God. Although God honored the desire of David's heart, because David was a man of much bloodshed, God would not allow him to build the Temple. The job would fall to Solomon, the King of Peace, the son of David.

Then King David rose to his feet and said, "Listen to me, my brethren and my people; I had intended to build a permanent home for the ark of the Covenant of the Lord and for the footstool of our God. So I made preparations to build it. But God said to me, 'You shall not build a house for My name because you are a man of war and have shed blood.' Yet, the Lord, the God of Israel, chose me from the all the house of my father to be king over Israel forever. For He has chosen Judah to be a leader; and in the house of Judah, my father's house, and among the sons of my father He took pleasure in me to make me king over all Israel. Of all my sons (for the Lord has given me many sons), He has chosen my son Solomon to sit on the throne of the kingdom of the Lord over Israel." (1 Chronicles 28:2-5).

Solomon was chosen to build the Temple to house the Ark. But Jesus *is* the true Solomon—the King of Peace. Jesus *is* the Temple. Jesus *is* the Ark. Jesus takes all of our sin and failure like the items inside the Ark. He takes our sin, bearing our sin in His body. The Mercy Seat covered over the sin of Israel. But His mercy takes our sin away entirely. The High Priest sprinkled the blood of a lamb upon the Mercy Seat, but Jesus—the great High Priest—sprinkles His own blood, which can truly take away sin. Like the Presence of God above the cherubim on the Ark, Jesus is surrounded by angels, and they worship Him (Hebrews 1:6). In the person of Jesus Christ, the Presence of God is truly above the mercy seat.

On account of His shed blood that was placed there, we have direct access into the very presence of God (Hebrews 10:19-20). We don't need to fear touching Him. His anger will not break out against us the way it did against Uzza, because the wrath of God has been satisfied on our behalf. Our sin is under the blood. His mercy was provided on the cross. We need only approach Him with reverence and accept His mercy by faith. Jesus is our Ark of Salvation. Just like Noah and his family escaped the judgment of God in an Ark, so an Ark was provided for our salvation. Jesus rescues us from our sins, lest we die. Come to His Mercy Seat and receive salvation.

CHAPTER 14

SEEN IN THE SLOW JUDGE

SECOND CHRONICLES

Second Chronicles begins at the zenith of Israel's prosperity and peace. The wise King Solomon is building the Temple, and even the surrounding nations are sending their best people and resources to assist him. Israel is in her glory. When the Temple is completed and the Ark of the Covenant is brought in, the glory of God literally fills the Temple. The house of the Lord "was filled with a cloud, so that the priests could not stand to minister because of the cloud, for the glory of the Lord filled the house of God" (2 Chronicles 5:13-14). Then Solomon offered a beautiful and powerful prayer of dedication (chapter 6). On this day, Israel was firing on all cylinders. The king and the nation were in step with God and His purposes. It was a time of overwhelming and unspeakable joy in the presence of the Living God.

Now when Solomon had finished praying, fire came down from heaven and consumed the burnt offering and sacrifices, and the glory of the Lord filled the house. The priests could not enter into the house of the Lord because the glory of the Lord filled the Lord's house. All the sons of Israel, seeing the fire come down and the glory of the Lord upon the house, bowed down on the pavement with their faces to the ground, and they worshipped and gave praise to the Lord, saying, "Truly He is good, truly His loving-kindness is everlasting" (2 Chronicles 7:1-3).

If only for this moment, Israel was exactly where they belonged, doing precisely what they were created to do. God was being glorified in them, and they were filled with joy. If only they could have stayed there, prostrated before God forever. But even before Solomon died, Israel began to drift away from God. Solomon reigned for 40 years in Jerusalem, and it was a time of peace and prosperity. But it would only go downhill from there.

On the day of the dedication of the Temple, God warned what would happen if Israel turned from God to follow other gods. If they did, then the purpose for which God created them would be jeopardized. They would misrepresent God to the nations. So God would have to exalt His Name among the nations by bringing judgment on His own people. He always desired for them to obey. He wanted them to choose life. But if they disobeyed (and chose death), then He would be glorified in His righteous judgment of the wicked.

But if you turn away and forsake my statutes and My commandments which I have set before you, and go and serve other gods and worship them, then I will uproot you from My land which I have given you, and this house which I have consecrated for My name I will cast out of My sight and I will make it a proverb and a byword among all peoples. As for this house, which was exalted, everyone who passes by it will be astonished and say, "Why has the Lord done thus to this land and to this house?" And they will say, "Because they forsook the Lord, the God of their fathers who brought them from the land of Egypt, and they adopted other gods and worshiped them and served them; therefore He has brought all this adversity on them" (2 Chronicles 7:19-22).

It did not take long for Israel to turn away from God. After the death of Solomon, because of the sinfulness of the people, God allowed the nation to be fractured down the middle. In actuality, ten tribes split to form the Northern Kingdom, and only Judah and Benjamin joined together in the south. But the Southern Kingdom had a Davidic King on the throne, whereas the Northern Kingdom was ruled by an imposter. In succession, the Northern Kings plunged Israel further and further into the worship of false gods.

In the south, the hearts of the people moved in the same direction. But much like the period of the Book of Judges, God would repeatedly send them a righteous Davidic King to pull the people out of the pit of their own sin. God was so long-suffering. Every time the people looked to Him for mercy, He granted it. But there had to come a point where His mercy gave way to judgment. When wickedness had overtaken both king and citizen, God's name would only be glorified by executing judgment.

The Book of 2 Chronicles is a story of descent into deeper and deeper levels of idolatry. But in the slowness of God to judge, we see an image of Jesus Christ. God must judge sin if He is a righteous God. The death of Jesus on the cross satisfied the righteous judgment of God against sin. His patience toward us, despite the number of times we have failed, reveals a love that far surpasses any other love the world has seen. Part of God's definition of *love* says, "love is patient . . ." (1 Corinthians 13:1). And He says, "In this is love, not that we loved God, but that He loved us and sent His Son to be the propitiation for our sins" (1 John 4:10).

Jesus is a Slow Judge. It is not His desire to punish us. He has done every possible thing to avert judgment. He even took it upon Himself. But as slow as He is, He must judge our sin. And if we persist in unbelief until the day we die, then time has run out. We will have to face the consequence on our own. How much wiser is it to trust Jesus Christ now, while there is still time?

Furthermore, all the officials of the priests and the people were very unfaithful following all the abominations of the nations; and they defiled the house of the Lord which He had sanctified in Jerusalem. The Lord, the God of their fathers, sent word to them again and again by His messengers, because He had compassion on His people and on His dwelling place; but they continually mocked the messengers of God, despised His words and scoffed at His prophets, until the wrath of the Lord rose against His people, until there was no remedy (2 Chronicles 36:14-16).

Jesus Christ is the remedy for sin. God sends His witnesses into all the world to tell everyone about the Remedy, but most reject Him. This is so sad, but it is not unexpected. "Enter through the narrow gate, for the gate is wide and the way is broad that leads to destruction, and there are many who enter through it. For the gate is small and the way is narrow that leads to life, and there are few who find it" (Matthew 7:13-14). The One whom we say is the Remedy is also the One who set this expectation.

Most people mock, despise and scoff at those of us who claim that Jesus is the only way to heaven. But the messengers have not spoken out of turn. Jesus clearly made this claim about Himself. He knew Himself to be the only Remedy because elsewhere He said, "I am the gate. Whoever enters through me will be saved" (John 10:9), and "I am the way, the truth, and the life. No one comes to the Father except through me" (John 14:6).

It is very important to me to be gentle and respectful when I tell people about the reasons why I have placed all my hope in Jesus Christ and why they should do the same. But given the danger that faces those who have not yet received the Remedy, how can I not also be direct and urgent? Isn't this the only loving thing to do? God has never been anything but entirely consistent. As He was with Israel, so He will be with His created ones today. "The wrath of the Lord rose against His people, until there was no remedy".

Jesus Christ died for you, dear friend. He has been so slow to judge. You and I are like Israel in the book of 2 Chronicles. We have turned away from God time and again, yet we benefit from the patience of the Slow Judge. But as Israel finally discovered, there comes a point where He will no longer stay His hand of judgment. How terrifying would it be to reach that point where there is no remedy? Why wait even another minute? Receive Jesus Christ—the only Remedy—now. Simply pray to God. Ask Him to forgive your sin on account of the sacrificial death of Jesus on the cross. Affirm your faith that Jesus arose from the dead. Ask Him to cleanse you from all sin by His atoning blood. Ask Him to put His Holy Spirit in you to change your heart. Call on the Name of Jesus to save you before His patience runs out.

CHAPTER 15

SEEN IN THE FAST FRIEND
EZRA

As slow as God is to drop the hammer of judgment, He is equally fast to extend to His friends the hand of His favor. This is the character of God as revealed throughout the Scriptures, and it is exactly the character that Jesus Christ demonstrated during His years on earth. One of my professors in Bible college always used to say, "you can't hide your character". He reminded us that character has a way of revealing itself over time. Moses—the "friend of God"—caught a glimpse of Yahweh's character when Moses heard God say, "The Lord, The Lord God, compassionate and gracious, slow to anger, and abounding in loving-kindness and truth" (Exodus 34:6). Moses knew that God is slow to judge and fast to befriend. And we see the same character, but now fully revealed in flesh and blood, in the person of Jesus Christ.

As we get to know Ezra, we find out that he is the great teacher of Israel, and this teacher enlightens us about Jesus Christ in at least two important ways. One, Ezra is a type of the greatest teacher in human history. The book of the Bible that bears Ezra's name sets at least one expectation for the coming Messiah, that He will be a great teacher. Two, what Ezra teaches us about Yahweh's character comes out in obvious ways in the words and works of Jesus Christ. Yahweh can't hide His character.

God was reluctant to send His people into captivity away from the Promised Land. He was reticent to destroy the Temple, which had been a house for the display of His glory and the exaltation of His name. It took several hundred years of worsening sin, idolatry, and rebellion before God's wrath rose and there was no longer any remedy. As He had warned, the people were expelled from the land for seventy years, one year for every Sabbath Year that they had ignored. The Israelites had been instructed to let their lands lay fallow every seventh year, but they completely ignored that command and never obeyed it. So we can calculate that God had been patient for 490 years. What a slow judge!

But equally as much, God proved to be a fast friend. The minute the Israelites' time in captivity had been fulfilled, God brought them back to the land and made provisions for the rebuilding of the Temple. Israel was God's friend, in His good graces, at the very minute of her repentance. God is so quick to forgive. And He pours out His favor upon His friends.

Ezra was a friend of God upon whom the favor of God was quickened. So much did Ezra's godliness rub off on the king of Persia that even the king threw himself completely behind Ezra's desire to see the Temple rebuilt. The king commissioned the work and even gave liberally to fund it. God's favor also rested upon the Israelites in order for them to successfully carry out the rebuilding work. We are repeatedly told Israel's success and especially Ezra's success was owed to the fact that "the good hand of his God was upon him" (Ezra 7:9). We can picture this "good hand", invisible though it is, as the favor of the Living God resting on Ezra's shoulder. God made Ezra His friend.

The quickness of Jesus to befriend humble people is striking in the New Testament. "Come follow me," He says to some simple fishermen, and they leave their nets to follow this compelling stranger. The outcast of a city, the despised Roman tax collector, climbs a tree to catch a glimpse of Jesus, and the Friend of sinners bids the man to come down from the tree and join Him for dinner. Religious leaders deride Him for eating with sinners. They are appalled when Jesus allows a prostitute to wash His feet with her tears and her hair. And an angry mob intent on stoning to death a woman caught in adultery is turned away as the woman finds a Friend who saves her life when she meets Jesus. As the mob looks on, His hand moves across the earth, His finger writing something in the sand. Then Jesus rises and says, "He who is without sin among you, let him be the first to throw a stone at her" (John 8:7).

One by one, they leave. But Jesus remains. He is truly sinless, so He alone could throw a stone. But He says, "neither do I condemn you" (John 8:11). Jesus extended His right hand of friendship to this woman the first time they met. She will no doubt be forever loyal.

But this is just the character of the man Jesus Christ. He is a fast Friend, even to sinners. As Yahweh was to Israel and Ezra in the book of Ezra, so Jesus was in the books of the New Testament. Jesus is an exact representation of the character of Yahweh.

The Book of Ezra also teaches us about Jesus Christ because the main character is an amazing teacher. It was not enough that Israel would have the physical place of worship back after the rebuilding of the Temple. Worship was a matter of the heart, and hammers and chisels would be of no use in changing hearts. Rather, words would be required, and not just clever words of human wisdom, but life-changing words that ultimately come from God. Ezra was a teacher of the word. The people flocked to him and he called them to repentance. 'As they responded, he methodically dealt with every individual, showing them a path to rid themselves of sin and walk in righteousness. What resulted was one of the great revivals of spiritual interest and commitment that the world has ever seen. But it began with something special about Ezra.

The good hand of his God was upon him. For Ezra had set his heart to study the law of the Lord and to practice it, and to teach His statutes and ordinances in Israel (Ezra 7:9).

Ezra was a great teacher because of his great love for the Word of God and his three-fold commitment to study, live, and teach. Had he not studied so well, he would not have known the Word of God. Had he not lived by its precepts, he would not have commanded the attention of Israel, who saw in Ezra a life consistent with the Word of God (Ezra 10:1). Had he not boldly taught the ways of God, then he would have remained alone in his practice of righteousness. But since he had all three, a great multitude responded to his teaching.

There is only one answer to the question that this raises. Who is the greatest teacher who has ever lived? Who is like Ezra, only greater? No school of thought (let alone any individual teacher) can a hold a candle to Jesus Christ in this regard. Two billion people alive today claim to take Him at His word. Empires and civilizations have been shaped by His words. John Winthrop preached His words while aboard the Arabella as pilgrims crossed the sea from Europe to America. Inspired by the words of Jesus, they dreamed of the colonies in America becoming a "City on a Hill". John Newton preached His words and brought down slavery in Britain. Abraham Lincoln and a thousand others did the same in America. Martin Luther King preached His words to bring equal rights to blacks in America. And today His words are transforming China, where conservative estimates say that there are 100 million believers who take Jesus at His word.

Even many who don't believe in Jesus know about His teaching. The words of Jesus, like "judge not, that ye be not judged" (Matthew 7:1), ring out from tattoo parlors and bumper stickers. His parables about a good Samaritan, a prodigal son, and a waiting father, inspire the world today. Who hasn't heard what Jesus said about forgiveness, turning the other cheek, loving your enemies, and praying for those who persecute you? Who doesn't know the Golden Rule? "Treat others the way you would like to be treated". Most people teach this to their children, although many do not know who it is they are quoting. The world has heard the words of Jesus, because He *is* the Word of God.

In the beginning was the Word and the Word was with God and the Word was God (John 1:1).

Jesus did not need to study the way Ezra did. He was there when "Let there be Light" (Genesis 1:3) rang out into the Universe. Like Ezra, and beyond him, Jesus practiced what He preached. He perfectly embodied what He said. And what Jesus taught changed the world and continues to do so. He taught us about the character of God, not only as one who has heard that God is the way He is, but as the God who is who He is. The book of Ezra reveals that the coming Messiah would be a fast friend of sinners and an amazing teacher. Jesus is the Friend of sinners, the perfect reflection of the character of God the Father, and the perfect teacher. Today, if you hear His voice, do not harden your heart, but listen to the Teacher.

CHAPTER 16

SEEN IN THE STRONG DEFENDER

NEHEMIAH

The greatest miracle that the world has seen since the resurrection and ascension of Jesus Christ is the endurance of Christians through persecution. Under Roman Emperors such as Nero, Domitian, Valerian, and Diocletian, the early believers suffered ten great waves of unspeakable persecution. Thousands upon thousands of Christians were burned at the stake, thrown to the lions in the Coliseum, beheaded, or killed through other forms of torture.

Another enormous wave of persecution broke out in Europe prior to the Reformation and during it. And as the Gospel has moved to the ends of the earth during the last two hundred years, more Christians have been martyred than ever before. As I write, just a couple of weeks ago, forty Christians were beheaded in North Korea for preaching about Jesus. Yet for all the suffering, something miraculous invariably takes place. Christians look death in the face, usually refuse an offer to spare their own lives by recanting their faith, and die courageously.

The miracle of how Christians die under persecution always made an impression on the nations that persecute them. Christians became known for their love for one another, for their equal concern for all people, and for their utter lack of fear in the face of death. It was even said that "the blood of the martyrs was the seed of the church", because the more people observed the death of believers, although their flesh trembled, their spirits were quickened by the clear demonstration that there is reason to have hope in a resurrection from the dead and life after death.

God was a defender even to those who died because Jesus' words gave them the courage to endure short-term pain and enjoy eternal delight. "Do not fear those who kill the body but are unable to kill the soul; but rather fear Him who is able to destroy both soul and body in hell" (Matthew 10:28). Believers thought that their momentary trials were not worth comparing with the eternal glory that was soon to be revealed. What's more, Jesus supernaturally comforted them in their affliction as He had promised to do. "I am with you always, even to the end of the age" (Matthew 28:20). Those who killed the Christians could only see the inexplicable joy on the faces of the believers. But those who suffered experienced the very presence of the Living God with them in those moments.

Sometimes God allows Christians to suffer. He always has a purpose in it, although we may not always be able to identify what it is. Our confidence comes from knowing Him well enough to trust

Him to work out His purposes and to do so for our good (Romans 8:28). But the moments of suffering that Christians sometimes endure do not nullify the reality that Jesus is our strong defender.

By in large, the world will always hate Christians. But Christians will always cling to Jesus and find in Him a refuge to run into. Jesus is like a fortified city. His walls protect us from the hostilities of the world. Whether they come in the form of murderous rage, like that of Adolf Hitler so that Christians like Corrie Ten Boom would cling to Jesus for dear life, or if they come in the form of subtle temptation toward worldly desires, like greed and jealousy, Christians can turn to Jesus, and He always defends us. As soon as we run to Him, we find safety. The Book of Nehemiah pictures Jerusalem as a city without walls and under the constant threat of great persecution. God sends Nehemiah to build Israel's walls of protection.

Hanani, one of my brothers, and some men from Judah came; and I asked them concerning the Jews who had escaped and had survived the captivity, and about Jerusalem. They said to me, "The remnant there in the province who survived the captivity are in great distress and reproach, and the wall to Jerusalem is broken down and its gates are burned with fire" (Nehemiah 1:2-3).

When Nehemiah hears about the plight of the Jews, he weeps and mourns, but also prays that God would send him to rebuild the walls. Nehemiah was in a unique position in the court of the Persian king. God moves the heart of the king, so the king sends Nehemiah on a mission to rebuild the walls of Jerusalem. Since Nehemiah is yet another type of Christ, in a similar way, as Jesus looked out over Jerusalem, He wept and said, "Behold your house is being left to you desolate!" (Matthew 23:38). Jesus then entered the city, only to be taken *outside the walls* and crucified there.

In so doing, Jesus became a Rescue for sinners, a wall of protection for those of us who are ruined by sin. The wrath of the Father could rise up at any moment and destroy the sinner, but those who have a wall of protection, a Defense from the One who can throw both soul and body in hell, are safe forever. Someone made a movie to mock Christians for our claim that we are "saved" (the name of the movie was "Saved"), but the reality is that Jesus *is* a Shield to those who believe in Him. We are forever safe in Him. As Nehemiah organized the believers to rebuild the walls, they were mocked the same way Christians are mocked today.

Now it came to pass that when Sanballat heard that we were rebuilding the wall, he became furious and very angry and mocked the Jews. He spoke in the presence of his brothers and the wealthy men of Samaria and said, "What are these feeble Jews doing? Are they going to restore it for themselves? Can they offer sacrifices? Can they finish in a day? Can they revive the stones from the dusty rubble even the burned ones?" Now Tobiah the Ammonite was near him and he said, "Even what they are building—if a fox should jump on it, he would break their stone wall down!" (Nehemiah 4:1-3).

Sanballat and Tobiah began to look for opportunities to raid the city. However, Nehemiah arranged a system of surveillance whereby the Jews could sound an alarm and everyone would rally to the point of attack. "As for the builders, each wore his sword girded at his side as he built, while the trumpeter stood near me" (Nehemiah 4:18). In an astonishingly short amount of time, the walls of the city of

Jerusalem were rebuilt, and the city had protection from her enemies.

In the same way, Jesus literally built the walls of our protection in a day—Good Friday, 33 AD. "Can they offer sacrifices? Can they finish in day?" Jesus offered His own body as a sacrifice, once and for all. On that day, He protected us from the death penalty that we deserve on account of our sinfulness. You see, before we come under the Protection of Jesus' Body, we are like Sanballat and Tobiah.

Then the soldiers of the governor took Jesus into the Praetorium and gathered the whole Roman cohort around Him. They stripped Him and put a scarlet robe on Him. And after twisting together a crown of thorns, they put it on His head, and a reed in His right hand, and they knelt down before Him and mocked Him, saying, "Hail, King of the Jews!" They spat on Him, and took the reed and began to beat Him on the head. After they had mocked Him, they took the scarlet robe off Him and put His own garments back on Him, and led Him away to crucify Him (Matthew 27:27-31).

We were not there on the day they crucified the Lord, but our mocking voices called out among the scoffers. As Sanballat and Tobiah spoke ahead of time, we still speak after the fact. Jesus said, "But I tell you that every careless word that people speak, they shall give an accounting for it in the day of judgment. For by your words you will be justified, and by your words you will be condemned" (Matthew 12:36-37). Every time we make fun of another person who was made in the image of God, we condemn ourselves. Every time we cast aspersions on the Bible—the very Word of God—we heap up condemnation upon ourselves. Every angry outburst, every hurtful dig, every lie, every careless word is like the mockery of the

Ammonite and the Roman. We are no different from them. And the same good promise extends to Jew and Gentile alike.

But what does it say? "The Word is near you, in your mouth and in your heart"—that is, the word of faith which we are preaching, that if you confess with your mouth Jesus as Lord, and believe in your heart that God raised Him from the dead, you will be saved (Romans 10:8-9).

The same mouth you once used to mock Jesus' claim to be King is now the instrument that you must use in order to be saved. Perhaps you laughed along with the mockers who made the movie "Saved". Maybe you never saw it, but you have mouthed the words "Oh My God" without meaning to revere His Holy Name. Have you used "Jesus Christ" as an expression of your disgust? People don't say "Buddha" when they hit their finger with a hammer. *Jesus* continues to be the object of the world's scorn, and Christians with Him, but it is time to repent and agree with His claim to be King. "Therefore everyone who confesses Me before men, I will also confess him before My Father who is in heaven. But whoever denies Me before men, I will also deny him before My Father who is in heaven" (Matthew 10:32-33). Jesus is therefore the Strong Defender of those who place their trust in Him. Nehemiah built the walls of Jerusalem, but Jesus built the walls of our salvation.

CHAPTER 17

SEEN IN THE GREAT REVERSAL
ESTHER

The purpose of this book—"Faith is not Blind"—is to demonstrate from Moses and the Prophets (meaning the 39 books of the Hebrew Bible) that Jesus is the Son of God who died on the cross and rose from the dead. It is my understanding that what Christians call the Old Testament is the primary evidence that we have in order to prove the claims of the New Testament. The 27 books of the New Testament explicitly reveal Jesus Christ, but He was already implied through the types, shadows, and prophecies that were given ahead of time. In this way, everything that came to pass in the New Testament is shown to be from God, because who but God knows the future? The Book of Esther is like one of the parables of Jesus. It reveals a great reversal resulting in the salvation of those the world scorns and the damnation of those the world esteems.

The Book of Esther is about a simple Jewish girl, whose ethnicity is unknown to those in power, who rises to be Queen of

Persia. A wicked hater of the Jews devises a plot to destroy the Jews. It is striking how many of these haters of the Jews there have been throughout the history of the world, including today. This man named Haman creates a genocidal plan that is set to go in motion. However with amazing courage, the Queen puts her own life at risk to save her people. That willingness to sacrifice herself for her people is typical of Christ. "And thus I will go into the king, which is not according to the law; and if I perish, I perish" (Esther 4:16). As it unfolds, the king does not kill her, but instead discovers the true nature of Haman's plot. Haman is hung on the gallows that he intended for his main Jewish rival—Mordecai. And the Jewish people are saved. The story is true, but it is also a parable for later that reveals how Jesus will reverse the destructive plans of Satan, bringing damnation upon wicked oppressors and salvation to many whom the world considers cursed. Jesus' own parable illustrates the reversal best.

Now there was a rich man, and he habitually dressed in purple and fine linen, joyously living in splendor every day. And a poor man named Lazarus was laid at his gate, covered with sores, and longing to be fed with the crumbs which were falling from the rich man's table; besides, even the dogs were coming and licking his sores. Now the poor man died and was carried away by the angels to Abraham's bosom; and the rich man also died and was buried. In Hades he lifted up his eyes, being in torment, and saw Abraham far away and Lazarus in his bosom. And he cried out and said, "Father Abraham, have mercy on me, and send Lazarus so that he may dip the tip of his finger in water and cool off my tongue, for I am in agony in this flame." But Abraham said, "Child, remember that during your life you received your good things, and likewise Lazarus bad things; but now he is being comforted here, and you are in agony. And besides all this, between us and you there is a great chasm fixed, so that those who wish to come over from here to you will not be able, and that none may cross over from there to us." And he said, "Then I beg you, father, that you send him to my father's house—for I have five brothers—in order that he may warn them, so that they will not also come to this place of torment." But Abraham said, "They have Moses and the Prophets; let them hear them." But he said, "No, father Abraham, but if someone goes to them from the dead, they will repent!" But he said to him, "If they do not listen to Moses and the Prophets, they will not be persuaded even if someone rises from the dead" (Luke 16:19-31).

Notice the great reversals in Jesus' story. The rich man ends up poor, and the poor ends up rich. The suffering ends up comforted, and the compassionless ends up suffering. The bossy one gets ignored, and the ignored one receives attention. The one who loved this world hates the next, but the one for whom this world held nothing gets everything in the next.

Does it follow then that heaven and hell are merely reversals of the states of men and women while they were on earth? No it does not, because there is a reversal offered to people before we die. Salvation is the greatest reversal that can happen in a person's life. Jesus used the expression "born again" to describe how drastic the changes are. Every person naturally lives for the world into which he is born. He pursues his self-interest, wanting to be happy. But when a person is born again, he dies to this world. He finds joy, but not in the things of this world. He finds life, but not what the world calls life. Whether the Christian is rich or poor in terms of this world's wealth, his life becomes Jesus Christ, so he lives for what pleases his Lord. Salvation is a great reversal away from a life oriented around the world to a life oriented around the Word.

The Author of our salvation also brought amazing reversals as He judged the world and saved it at the same time. He judged those who would ultimately reject Him, but He saved anyone who would ultimately believe in Him. Consider the cross. It was the worst form of torture that humanity had devised. But God reversed the meaning of it and turned it into the hope of the world's salvation. Consider the crown of thorns. The world wove it and pressed it upon Jesus to mock His claim to be King, but He wore the crown as a suffering servant who takes the sin of the world upon His head, showing the world the true meaning of what it is to be King. Consider the nails. The world stretched Jesus out to make Him appear helpless, but His arms were stretched out in that way in order to say to the world, "'Come'. And let the one who hears say, 'Come'. And let the one who is thirsty come; let the one who wishes take the water of life without cost'" (Revelation 22:17). The nails held open the door of salvation.

Satan plotted the death of the Son of David the way that Haman plotted the death of Mordecai and all the Jews. But God hung Satan on his own gallows. Satan struck Jesus with a death wound through the heel into the cross, but in that death, Jesus crushed the head of the serpent. Jesus died to save the people that Satan hates. Haman was therefore an anti-Christ, and Mordecai was a type of Christ. But the story of Esther, like the story of the Rich Man and Lazarus, has a message about us as well. Like Esther, we must be willing to perish. If we try to hold on to the riches of this world, "the worry of the world and the deceitfulness of wealth" as Jesus said in Matthew 13:22, then we are in danger of losing our souls for all eternity.

And He summoned the crowd with His disciples, and said to them, "If anyone wishes to come after Me, he must deny himself, and take up his cross and follow me. For whoever wishes to save his life will lose it, but whoever loses his life for My sake and the Gospel's will save it. For what does it profit a man to gain the whole world, and forfeit his soul? For what will a man give in exchange for his soul? For whoever is ashamed of Me and My words in this adulterous and sinful generation, the Son of Man will also be ashamed of him when He comes in the glory of His father with the holy angels" (Mark 8:34-38).

There is a great reversal offered to us now on this side of death. We can let go of what this world has to offer. We can ignore what haters will say, even if it is our own mother or father. We can take hold of the Life that is really Life. We can flee the entrapments of this world in order to take hold of Jesus Christ. If we do, then we will enjoy eternal life in heaven with Him.

But if we die in our sins, having lived this life for whatever it had to offer, then we will end up like Haman and the rich man of Jesus' parable. As the parable reminds us, we have Moses and the Prophets. These 39 books were written for our benefit, to give us reason to believe the Gospel. If you will not listen to Moses and the Prophets, then would you listen even if someone rose from the dead? Jesus did rise from the dead! So we have the testimony made even more certain. Why not let go of the concerns of this world and believe in the foolishness of the Gospel? Paradoxically, the One nailed to a cross dying with a crown of thorns upon His head is our only hope for experiencing eternal life.

CHAPTER 18

SEEN IN THE SUFFERING INNOCENT

JOB

The sufferings of Job are well known, but sadly, so many people miss how they point to Jesus Christ. Yet the Book of Job speaks loudly. Job was "blameless, upright, fearing God and turning away from evil" (Job 1:1), not literally, but enough to represent the sinlessness of the Son of God. Job was hated by Satan and allowed by God to suffer, just like the Son of God. He cried out to God in the midst of his pain as Jesus also cried to His Father. "Father, if you are willing, take this cup from me" (Luke 22:42). "My God! My God! Why have you forsaken Me?" (Matthew 27:46).

The Book of Job serves an important function in the overall narrative of redemption that we find in the Bible. It reveals that not everyone who suffers does so on account of his own sin. After reading Job, as we consider the death of Jesus Christ, we should not be surprised that such a fiery trial came upon our Savior. We should not doubt that He is the most righteous of all when we see Him suffer more than any man.

Job suffered the loss of all of his possessions and the death of all of his children. His wife remained alive with him, but she turned on him, advising him to "curse God and die!" (Job 2:9). Some of his friends came from afar, and commendably, they sat with him in his agony, wept with him, and said nothing. But soon they began to speak. The foolishness they spouted had an air of wisdom, but in actuality, it was foolishness that needed to be exposed for what it is. Most people today think the way Job's friends did, and this is a part of their resistance to the Gospel.

Eliphaz explained that the innocent do not suffer. Bildad said that God rewards the good. Zophar rebuked Job for failing to see the supposed wisdom of the others. In the same way, the world teaches a do-good religion that has these elements in common. Whether it is Buddhism with its 8-fold path, Judaism with its 10 Commandments, Islam with its 5 Pillars, Catholicism with its 10 work requirements, or another system with their list of what makes a person good, all do-good religion connects God's reward with human beings doing good. According to this human tradition, suffering is reserved for those who do bad, and reward (ultimately heaven or Nirvana or the like) is for those whose good outweighs their bad.

So Job's friends had one explanation to offer him: that is, Job must have sinned and brought this calamity upon himself. Job knew that there had to be another reason for his suffering, but eventually he slipped into thinking along the same lines as his friends were. He begins to try to prove them wrong by appealing to his own righteousness. Thankfully, and majestically, God finally speaks for Himself near the end of the book of Job.

Then the Lord answered Job out of the whirlwind and said, "Who is this that darkens counsel by words without knowledge?"(Job 38:1-2).

God goes on to remind Job of the vastness and grandeur of creation. He reminds him that God alone was there in the beginning. He alone knows everything, and the questions that Job and his friends thought they could adequately answer turn out to be above their pay grade.

Then Job replied to the LORD: "I know that You can do all things; no purpose of Yours can be thwarted. You asked, 'Who is this that obscures My plans without knowledge?' Surely I spoke of things I did not understand, things too wonderful for me to know. "You said, 'Listen now, and I will speak; I will question you, and you shall answer Me.' My ears had heard of You but now my eyes have seen You. Therefore I despise myself and repent in dust and ashes" (Job 42:1-6).

The Book of Job brings the reader to dust and ashes next to Job. It empties us of all of our preconceptions about what God has to do. The truth is that He does not have to reward us for being as good as we try to be. Whatever system of righteousness that we think can compel God to bless us is worthless in the presence of His holiness. Job was not perfectly righteous, and neither are we. God owes us nothing, and our efforts to be good cannot save us.

The Book of Job also speaks to the suffering of Jesus Christ. The reason for His suffering is far beyond our human reasoning.

Many of the religious elite during Jesus' day were convinced that Jesus must have been a sinner since God allowed Him to suffer the way He did. Even today, Muslims will say that God put the traitor Judas to suffer in the place of Jesus because God would never allow His holy prophet to suffer the way Jesus did.

But the Book of Job empties us of the folly of such thinking. "No purpose of God's can be thwarted" (Job 42:2). If it was the Father's will to crush His own Son in the place of wicked sinners, although His Son is Himself innocent, then who are we to question the purposes of God? Job was right to realize what he did in the end. "Therefore I have declared that which I did not understand, things too wonderful for me, which I did not know".

In the midst of Job's suffering, he cried out for an advocate. What he didn't know was that he was crying out for Jesus. "For He is not a man as I am that I may answer Him, that we may go to court together. There is no umpire between us, who may lay his hand upon us both. Let Him remove His rod from me, and let not dread of Him terrify me. Then I would speak and not fear Him; But I am not like that in myself" (Job 9:32-35).

Who is a man like we are human? Who could go to court with us? Who could be an Umpire, a perfect Judge for God and a perfect Advocate for Man? Who can remove the rod of God's discipline? Who can open the way for us to speak to God? Who can remove our fear of judgment? Who can do for me what I cannot do for myself? Jesus Christ is this Umpire for which Job longed! He is all of those things for us. He was there for Job, although Job did not know it at the time.

Jesus Christ is the Suffering Innocent, afflicted by God but not for His own sin. Jesus Christ makes a way to the Father that human religion couldn't find. The wisdom of God confounds the answers of men. Man speaks for thirty or more chapters in the Book of Job, but God speaks in the end, and He alone is able to reveal His own mysterious way. Our part is not to be wise in our own eyes, but to receive what God has revealed. And the Book of Job reveals the Suffering Innocent who serves as a perfect Umpire between God and Man, for He is both. He calls us to repent in dust and ashes and humbly take Him at His Word.

CHAPTER 19

SEEN IN THE FORSAKEN
PSALMS

Psalms contains what is in my estimation the most amazing prophecy of Jesus Christ that God gave us. It is Psalm 22. It comes just before what is one of the most loved chapters in the Bible, "The Lord is my shepherd . . ." Psalm 23 also points us to Jesus Christ because Jesus made the explicit claim, "I am the Good Shepherd. The Good Shepherd lays down His life for His sheep" (John 10:11). In addition to Psalm 22 and 23, there are dozens of other specific references to the coming Messiah in the book of Psalms. Psalm 110 is the most quoted of all Old Testament Scripture by the New Testament. Jesus Himself used it to confound His questioners.

"What do you think about the Christ, whose Son is He?" They said to Him, "The son of David." He said to them, "Then how does David in the Spirit call Him 'Lord', saying, 'The Lord said to my Lord, "Sit at My right hand, until I put your enemies beneath your feet"? If David then calls him 'Lord', how is he his son?" (Matthew 22:41-45).

The answer to Jesus' riddle is that Jesus is the son of David because Jesus is fully human, having descended from David, but Jesus is also fully God and rightfully addressed as Lord. David spoke prophetically about the coming Messiah. This is in fact the only good explanation for Psalm 110:1. When Jesus showed this to the Pharisees, we are told that "No one was able to answer Him a word, nor did anyone dare from that day on to ask Him another question" (Matthew 22:46). The Priests didn't know it at the time, but they were examining the Passover Lamb to see if He was spotless. That all of their questions were put to rest was evidence that the Lamb has been proven to be blameless. But as I said, they didn't understand it at the time. And still today, no one can understand the answer to Jesus' question unless they are willing to confess that He is Lord, for this is the only explanation.

Psalm 110 is also an important Messianic Psalm because it reveals how it is that Jesus is a Priest. As discussed in the chapter on Genesis, Jesus is a Priest according to the order of Melchizedek (Psalm 110:4). Next, Psalm 2 pictures the Messiah as the King of Israel and of the world. "Serve the Lord with fear and celebrate His rule with trembling. Kiss His son, or He will be angry and your way will lead to your destruction, for His wrath can flare up in a moment. Blessed are all who take refuge in Him" (Psalm 2:10-12).

Additionally, Psalm 16 is important because it speaks about the resurrection of David before his body is allowed to see decay. But David dies and his body does see decay, so the New Testament rightly points out that the Psalm actually spoke of the Son of

David—Jesus Christ—whose body was buried, but not long enough to see decay. All of these Psalms are striking. In fact, the word "salvation" appears more than sixty times in the Psalms. Since Jesus' name means "Yahweh is salvation", it is clear that many of the Psalms are pointing to Him. But Psalm 22 is so striking that, even by itself, it should inspire faith in the hearer. Faith is not blind. Faith is the normal response to revelation like this.

Hanging on the cross, Jesus only uttered seven short sayings. One of them, the most agonized cry of them all, was a direct quote of Psalm 22:1. "My God! My God! Why have you forsaken me?" By quoting this verse, Jesus wasn't asking God for information that He didn't know. Jesus knew why crucifixion was happening to Him. Rather, He quoted the first verse in order that we who hear what He said on the cross would read what was written and believe that the crucifixion of God's Son was God's long foretold plan to save the world, especially those who will believe.

When David wrote these words around the year 1000 BC, Rome was still hundreds of years away from rising as an Empire. So David could not have encountered Roman crucifixion. The first historical record of crucifixion didn't appear until 519 BC when Darius, the King of Persia, crucified 3000 people. But David was a Prophet, and although he wrote half a millennium before the invention of crucifixion, he spoke clearly of the crucifixion of Messiah.

On the cross, Jesus directed us to read Psalm 22, and as we do, we discover that there are 22 amazing indications of the kind of rejection and death that Messiah would suffer:

1. He would cry out, "My God! My God! Why have you forsaken me?" (22:1).
2. The Father would not answer, but would separate Himself from the cries of His Son (22:1-2).
3. This agonizing separation would include a night and day of the Son crying out to no avail (22:2).
4. The forsaken Son would continue to affirm the holiness and trustworthiness of the Father in the midst of His being forsaken (22:3-5).
5. The Son would be mocked and sneered at. "They separate with the lip, they wag the head, saying, 'Commit yourself to the Lord; Let Him deliver him; Let Him rescue him, because He delights in him'" (22:6-8).
6. Yet the Son will have been specially set apart to God even from birth (22:9-10).
7. Trouble will press in violently from all sides. "Many bulls have surrounded me; strong bulls of Bashan have encircled me" (22:11-12).
8. The encircling men will intimidate with harsh words. "They open wide their mouth at me, as a ravening and roaring lion" (22:13).
9. He will bleed and dehydrate. "I am poured out like water" (22:14a).
10. His bones will not be broken, but pulled out of socket. "All my bones are out of joint" (22:14b).
11. His heart will strain until it begins to fail and shut down. "My

heart is like wax; It is melted within me" (22:14c).

12. As strength dries up, His tongue will literally cleave to the roof of His mouth (22:15).
13. He will again be encircled. "For dogs have surrounded me; a band of evildoers has encompassed me" (22:16a).
14. "They pierced my hands and my feet" (22:16b). Crucifixion literally pierces the hands and feet.
15. "I can count all my bones" (22:17a). Crucifixion stretches out and exposes the body.
16. "They look, they stare at me" (22:17b). Crucifixion elevates the person for public viewing.
17. "They divide my garments among them, and for my clothing they cast lots" (22:18).
18. After being laid "in the dust of death", He will then be delivered from His attackers (22:19-21).
19. He will yet again tell of God's Name and call forth worshippers (22:22-23).
20. Although it appeared that God had not heard since the Son was allowed to suffer, "He has not despised nor abhorred the affliction of the afflicted" (22:24).
21. The afflicted will once again eat with those who believe in Him and praise Him (22:25-26).
22. "All the ends of the earth will remember and turn to the Lord . . . They will come and will declare His righteousness to a people who will be born, that He has performed it" (22:27-31).

If someone has never read the four eyewitness accounts of the crucifixion of Jesus (those recorded by Matthew, Mark, Luke, and John), he or she may not recognize how amazing the 22 prophecies of Psalm 22 really are. But they are so specific, so detailed, that they cannot be overlooked. Remember that crucifixion was 500 years away from being invented when the Psalm was written. Yet it is as if David is there in 33AD, witnessing Jesus being forsaken.

Put yourself there in Jerusalem at the Passover Festival in 33 AD, but do so with Psalm 22 in mind. Can you hear Jesus' cry to the Father? Why doesn't the Father answer? Why are these Roman soldiers allowed to surround and mock the Messiah? They pierce Him through His hands and His feet with nails, just as the Psalmist predicted. Do the mockers have it right when they say, "if you are the Son of God, then come down from that cross"? His tongue cleaves to the roof of His mouth, so He can hardly form the words "I thirst". A soldier uses his spear to lift a sponge soaked in vinegar to his lips. Jesus heaves on the cross, lifting up to get air, then slouching back down again. His heart is failing.

Meanwhile, the soldiers divide His clothes among them. Coming to the robe, they decide it is of greater value if not torn, so they cast lots to decide who will get to take it home. On the cross, Jesus' ribs are visible through His skin. You can count them. His shoulders are out of joint from the stretching of His arms upon the cross. A crowd surrounds Him on Golgotha. Some gloat over Him. A few worship. He breathes his last, and a soldier thrusts a spear through His side to assure that He is dead. They lay Him in the dust of death.

Three days later, the Son of God is vindicated as He rises from the dead. The Father has accepted the suffering of the forsaken Son of God as a once-for-all payment for sin. Jesus appears to His disciples and even eats fish with them on the beach and in an inner room. They stop doubting and believe. After His ascension, they go out into all the world and preach the good news of Jesus' death and resurrection to all who will hear. And they do hear. From generation to generation and on every continent, the Name of Jesus is lifted high and exalted.

Psalm 22 gave us 22 reasons to believe that the story is true. No other explanation can fit what is plainly revealed. It was always the plan of the Father to lay the sin of the world upon His Son. After His suffering, He would be believed upon in the world. As Jesus asked, "What do you think about the Christ, whose Son is He?"

CHAPTER 20

SEEN IN THE WORD

PROVERBS

Solomon is known as the wisest man who has ever lived. That is probably true, unless Jesus Christ is included among those being considered. Solomon had a unique gift of wisdom partly because he was a type of Jesus Christ. Solomon was the son of David whom God chose to demonstrate what the Kingdom of God would bring. His name means "King of Peace", and his reign brought a peace and prosperity that gave us a glimpse of what the reign of Jesus will bring. His wisdom gives us a glimpse of the wisdom of Jesus. Solomon is the primary author of the book of Proverbs, which contains thirty-one chapters of divine wisdom, mostly in the form of short pithy statements. These sayings help us understand life and give guidance to life. Since knowing Jesus Christ is the meaning of life, they naturally point to Him.

In the New Testament, Jesus is called the Word. The Greek word "Logos", from which we get "logic", refers to divine reason or created order. When Jesus is given this title, it is often with reference to His being present at the moment of creation. John explicitly says that He is not wisdom, as in created order, but is the eternal uncreated instrument through which the created order came into being.

In the beginning was the Word, and the Word was with God, and the Word was God. He was in the beginning with God. All things came into being through Him, and apart from Him nothing came into being that has come into being (John 1:1-3).

So, Jesus is the author of wisdom, and thus, the ultimate author of the Book of Proverbs. It is impossible to truly be wise if one rejects Jesus. Someone may be smart and may know a vast amount of information. But if he or she rejects the author of wisdom, demonstrating no fear of God, which is the beginning of wisdom (Proverbs 1:7), then he or she is foolish.

Surely I am more stupid than any man, and I do not have the understanding of a man. Neither have I learned wisdom, nor do I have the knowledge of the Holy One. Who has ascended into heaven and descended? Who has gathered the wind in His fists? Who has wrapped the waters in His garments? Who has established all the ends of the earth? What is His name or His son's name? Surely you know! (Proverbs 30:2-4).

Since God is the author of wisdom, and since He created everything, including wisdom, through His Son, it is not surprising that we find Jesus speaking unparalleled wisdom. Jesus is famous for His parables. He would teach truth using illustrations that people understood from their everyday lives. He spoke of fishermen with their dragnets, farmers sowing seed, and a woman searching desperately for a lost coin in her home. The truth that these parables conveyed was penetrating. Those who heard marveled at the way Jesus spoke. They could hardly believe that He was the son of an ordinary carpenter, not trained in the elite religious schools. "Where did this man get this wisdom?" (Matthew 13:54)

The answer to their question was that He created it. He was the author of wisdom. When He spoke parables, it was from His heart, the fountain of all wisdom. In fact, the Greek word for "parable" is really a translation of the Hebrew word for "proverb". When Solomon wrote the Book of Proverbs, it was Jesus who gave him the words. When Jesus spoke parables, He was able to do so because He is the Word of God.

Believing in Jesus is called "becoming wise unto salvation" or receiving "the wisdom that leads to salvation" (2 Timothy 3:15). True wisdom comes from God. A simple child can be wiser than the most educated adult if the former acknowledges the Son of God while the latter does not. Attaining wisdom requires that we hear from God. "God, after He spoke long ago to the fathers in the prophets in many portions and in many ways, in these last days has spoken to us in His Son, whom He appointed heir of all things, through whom also He made the world" (Hebrews 1:1-2).

To the educated Greek, this proposition that wisdom begins with confessing Jesus as Lord was highly insulting. It did not esteem their intellect the way they would have liked. It wasn't that the message was anti-intellectual, but it was supra-intellectual. It required more than one's intellect. Individuals could not arrive at the Truth simply through their own human reasoning. They depended on God revealing this truth. Although it is humbling to those who think themselves wise, God had a purpose in subjugating man's wisdom to His wisdom, just as He has a purpose in everything.

For the word of the cross is foolishness to those who are perishing, but to us who are being saved it is the power of God. For it is written, "I will destroy the wisdom of the wise, and the cleverness of the clever I will set aside." Where is the wise man? Where is the scribe? Where is the debater of this age? Has not God made foolish the wisdom of the world? For since in the wisdom of God the world through its wisdom did not come to know God, God was well-pleased through the foolishness of the message preached to save those who believe. For indeed Jews ask for signs and Greeks search for wisdom; but we preach Christ crucified, to Jews a stumbling block and to Gentiles foolishness, but to those who are called, both Jews and Greeks, Christ the power of God and the wisdom of God. Because the foolishness of God is wiser than men, and the weakness of God is stronger than men (1 Corinthians 1:18-25).

Faith ultimately comes down to trusting the revelation of God. The Truth of the Scriptures will rise to the top when a reader approaches them humbly. Finding Truth must begin there—with a healthy fear of the Lord. The teachings of the wisest man who ever lived—Jesus Christ—will commend themselves to the humble. Solomon took pride in his intellect, but that pride eventually led to his fall. There is a certain wisdom in humility, especially being willing to be a fool for Christ. The Gospel doesn't bow to human reasoning. Since it is true, it is entirely consistent with reality. But since it takes special revelation from God in order to be known, it is entirely offensive to those who applaud themselves for their own independent thought. Are you willing to trust the words of Another, even if it means that you can't be wise in your own eyes or in the eyes of the world?

CHAPTER 21

SEEN IN THE MEANING OF LIFE
ECCLESIASTES

The wise King Solomon at one point struggled with depression as he contemplated the meaning of life. Although he had it all, it all began to appear meaningless. "Vanity of vanities! All is vanity" (Ecclesiastes 1:2). Solomon contemplated how there is nothing really new under the sun. He considered his own wisdom and lamented that "in much wisdom is much grief" (1:18). He experimented with pleasure and with the acquisition of possessions. But these also proved to be empty, only another form of vanity.

Solomon despaired even more when he considered that even the fruits of his productive labor might come into the hands of a fool when he died. Then he thought about the horrible reality of evil oppression on earth, and the thought of it was so overwhelming that "I congratulated the dead who are already dead more than the living who are still living" (4:2). All things considered, Solomon is right. This world is meaningless and not worth living. But God . . .

In the last chapter of Ecclesiastes, Solomon remembers God. Remembering Him gives meaning to life. As the years of a man wind to a close, the pleasures of this life increasingly give way to struggles of old age. Where then should we put our hope? Should we hope in this world or in the next? What's more, each of us faces the reality of death. Where then can we find hope?

Remember also your Creator in the days of your youth, before the evil days come and the years draw near when you will say, "I have no delight in them"; before the sun and the light, the moon and the stars are darkened, and clouds return after the rain . . . Remember Him before the silver chord is broken and the golden bowl is crushed, the pitcher by the well is shattered and the wheel at the cistern is crushed; then the dust will return to the earth as it was, and the spirit will return to God who gave it (Ecclesiastes 12:1-7).

If it were not for the resurrection of Jesus Christ from the dead, then surely all would indeed be vanity. The lives of men and women would only be a countdown to ultimate meaninglessness. But the resurrection of the dead offers the hope of ultimate meaning. Since Jesus conquered death, there is reason to believe that my life can avail to some ultimate purpose. Resurrection makes meaning in life possible. Martha was a friend of Jesus who was grieving the death of her brother. She believed in the resurrection of the dead, but she didn't fully understand that Jesus was not only the power that will one day accomplish the resurrection of the dead, but that as such, He makes life worth living on this side of death.

Martha then said to Jesus, "Lord, if you had been here, my brother would not have died. Even now I know that whatever you ask of God, God will give you." Jesus said to her, "Your brother will rise again." Martha said to Him, "I know that he will rise again in the resurrection on the last day." Jesus said to her, "I am the resurrection and the life, he who believes in Me will live even if he dies, and everyone who lives and believes in Me will never die. Do you believe this?" She said to Him, "Yes, Lord; I have believed that You are the Christ, the Son of God, even He who comes into the world" (John 11:21-27).

Jesus proceeded to resurrect Lazarus from the dead. This demonstration of power over death itself, and even more so, when Jesus brings Himself out of the tomb on the third day after His own death, proves the claim Jesus makes about Himself. Notice that He says more than that He is able to raise the dead. He claims to be able to give life—real life—that begins in the here and now and that continues on the other side of death. Physical death becomes nothing more than a transition from one state of being to another. And life becomes more than mere physical life. Life is defined as being *in Him*. Jesus says, "I am the resurrection and *the life*". The meaning of life, that which eluded Solomon in his desperate moments of contemplation, is to know the One whom God sent into the world. Martha would physically die, but she had real, lasting, eternal life that is undaunted by physical death because she had believed that Jesus is the Christ, the Son of God.

A few things mark the *real life* that Jesus alone can give. From deep within the person, like water coming up from a spring, **love** wells up. This is the first mark of being born from above. There is also a supernatural **joy**. It is beyond natural happiness because it doesn't depend upon outward circumstance. One can be shackled in a prison and sing joyful hymns from the bottom of his heart. There is also a **desire** for the Word of God, a desire to pray, a desire to obey and bring pleasure to the Lord Jesus. It is an experience that lasts, not just an emotional high, but a reality that continues to death and beyond. No descriptions of eternal life can adequately describe what it is like to know Jesus Christ. It is very personal and entirely real.

The world clamors to answer the question that plagued Solomon. What is the meaning of life? The meaning of life is to know Jesus Christ. Those who know Him will of necessity bring glory to the Father. The Creator of humankind made us for His own glory. And He is glorified by the obedience of faith. When a person trusts God, taking Him at His word, receiving the gift offered through the shedding of Jesus' blood, God is well pleased. He is glorified in us.

Simultaneously, we are satisfied in Him. Nothing else will fill that God-shaped hole in our hearts that was made a vacuum on the day of our sin. Only God can satisfy the human heart. He makes Himself known through Jesus Christ, so those who come to Him enter into the joy of the Lord. We were made for His glory in us, and our joy in Him.

My Father is glorified by this, that you bear much fruit, and so prove to be my disciples . . . These things I have spoken to you so that My joy may be in you, and that your joy may be made full (John 15:8-11).

Ecclesiastes calls us to honestly contemplate the meaning of life. It probes us, asking what we are living for. Then it exposes that these things are not able to bring life. If we are willing to think about it, then we discover that all is vanity. Everything is vanity. But God sent

His Son into the world to give life. The life He offers extends beyond the grave to all eternity. He alone offers ultimate meaning. He is the life. And He proved it by His resurrection from the dead. Jesus is the Resurrection and the Life.

CHAPTER 22

SEEN IN THE LOVING HUSBAND

SONG OF SOLOMON

Solomon gave us a representation of King Jesus. Solomon's name—King of Peace—was fitting because his kingdom brought peace throughout the land and even to surrounding nations. Jesus will soon return to bring a lasting Kingdom of Peace. The wisdom of Solomon, particularly in the book of Proverbs, points us to the Author of Wisdom—Jesus Christ. The Word of God, as He came to be called, spoke parables as Solomon spoke proverbs. But more than that, He is the wisdom of God. The world through its wisdom cannot know God. Rather, the wisdom of God is the message of Christ crucified. Those who believe the message become wise unto salvation.

Solomon's seemingly despairing book of Ecclesiastes also points us to salvation in Jesus Christ, because if Jesus is not the Resurrection and the Life, then Solomon is right. Everything is vanity, and we are just buying time until the dust of our flesh returns to the dust of the earth. So Solomon reveals Jesus Christ through his kingdom of peace, through his wisdom, and through his contemplation of the meaning of life. But there is yet one more way in which he makes Christ known.

There are different kinds of love. You do not love your mother the same way you love ice cream. The book called Song of Solomon is famous for its depiction of erotic love. Solomon and his wife have desires to be together physically. There are many allusions to this kind of love in the book, and it is done in a tasteful way, not inappropriately. Many people are surprised to find this in the Bible. But the clear message from Genesis onward is that this kind of love between a husband and a wife is part of God's design. It is good. But this is not the only kind of love that we find in the Song of Solomon. The Husband's love for his bride is not only sexual. He also has feelings of affection, loyalty, trust, friendship, and companionship for her. He desires to spend time with her simply because he loves her.

The New Testament presents Jesus as a loving husband. Contrary to how some people describe it, the Bible never speaks about Jesus being a loving husband to any individual. Rather, the analogy is always applied to His love for the Church. The bride of Christ is the group of all believers throughout the ages. When the Song of Solomon speaks of a wedding banquet, it pictures the marriage supper when Jesus finally receives His people to be with Him forever.

He has brought me to his banquet hall, and his banner over me is love (Song of Solomon 2:4).

Jesus' motivation for giving His life was love. By dying in our place, He took away the filthy rags of our sinful condition. He clothes us in His own righteousness. Our part is only to believe in Him. But from the moment of His death and resurrection until the moment when the final member of the Bride of Christ becomes a believer, there is a long time to wait. We are waiting for that day when He will bring us to His banquet hall, and His banner over us will be love. It will be a celebration like none that has ever gone before. Wedding ceremonies like Solomon's could only give us a glimpse of what that day will be like.

"Let us rejoice and be glad and give the glory to Him, for the marriage of the Lamb has come and His bride has made herself ready." It was given to her to clothe herself in fine linen, bright and clean; for the fine linen is the righteous acts of the saints. Then he said to me, "Write, 'Blessed are those who are invited to the marriage supper of the Lamb'". And he said to me, "These are true words of God"(Revelation 19:7-9).

The words of God are true, but many find them hard to accept. One of the great hindrances to faith is the belief that "God doesn't love me". But Song of Solomon presents a passionate man who truly desires to be with his bride. And the New Testament clearly calls each of us to be present at the coming banquet. The problem is not that God doesn't love any one of us. Rather, many of us refuse His invitation to the banquet.

But He said to him, "A man was giving a big dinner and he invited many; and at the dinner hour he sent his slave to say to those who had been invited, 'Come; for everything is ready now.' But they all alike began to make excuses . . . And the slave came back and reported this to his master. Then the head of the household became angry and said to his slave, 'Go out at once into the streets and lanes of the city and bring in here the poor and crippled and blind and lame.' And the slave said, 'Master, what you have commanded has been done, and still there is room.' And the Master said to the slave, 'Go out into the highways and along the hedges, and compel them to come in, so that my house may be filled. For I tell you, none of those men who were invited shall taste of my dinner'" (Luke 14:16-24).

I am a slave who was sent to invite you to come to the dinner banquet. Please don't make any excuses. The Master has prepared a table, and there is plenty of room there for you. Those who ultimately refuse him will not be allowed in once the doors are closed. The door of opportunity closes when Jesus returns or when a person dies, whichever comes first.

God's invitation does have this expiration date. But notice what motivated Him to throw a banquet for us in the first place. Notice how widely He extends a genuine invitation to whosoever is willing to come. He is a loving Husband who wants each of us to be members of the Bride. "For while we were still helpless, at the right time Christ died for the ungodly. For one will hardly die for a righteous man; though perhaps for the good man someone would dare even to die. But God demonstrates His own love for us, in that while we were yet sinners, Christ died for us" (Romans 5:6-8).

God doesn't ask that you be good enough to deserve to come to the dinner. He invites you simply because He loves you. Please come to the banquet table under the banner of Jesus' love.

CHAPTER 23

SEEN IN THE SUFFERING SERVANT
ISAIAH

The Book of Isaiah has 66 chapters, the same number as the Bible has books. The first 39 chapters of Isaiah parallel many of the themes of the Old Testament and the remaining 27 prefigure the main ideas of the New Testament. This provides some evidence that the God of the Old Testament always intended to provide the New when the fullness of time had come. But more importantly, there is a direct prophecy about the suffering servant found in this latter portion of Isaiah. One could not overstate the significance of Isaiah 52:13-53:12. Only Psalm 22 surpasses it in terms of the number of details about Jesus' death and resurrection. And like the book of Psalms, Isaiah is full of other prophecies about Jesus—too many than space will allow us to mention here. There are, however, three passages that must be mentioned before proceeding on with the suffering servant passage.

First, there is a prophecy about the virgin birth of Jesus. In context, Isaiah is speaking to King Ahaz, who refuses the prophet's command to ask God for a sign. As a rebuke, Isaiah says the following, but it applies to something far more significant than what applied to Ahaz.

Therefore the Lord Himself will give you a sign: Behold, a virgin will be with child and bear a son, and she will call His name Immanuel (Isaiah 7:14).

The prophecy was fulfilled in the time of Ahaz, because the Hebrew word for "virgin" can simply refer to a "young woman". But more significantly, it was fulfilled in a most supernatural way in the birth of Jesus 800 years later. That Jesus was born to a young woman who was also literally a virgin is a great sign that Jesus is unique among everyone who has ever been born of a woman. But that this Isaiah prophecy is written, and that it is still available to be viewed today in a manuscript that predates the birth of Jesus, namely the Great Isaiah Scroll of the Dead Sea Scrolls, is amazing evidence that Jesus is the Son of God. His virgin birth was predicted.

Not only so, there is a prophecy that speaks to the identity of Messiah, that He will be far more than an ordinary prophet. In fact the prophecy says it outright that the Messiah will *be* God! The prophecy begins with an important image of Messiah being like Light shining in a dark place. "The people who walk in darkness will see a great Light; those who live in a dark land, the Light will shine on them" (Isaiah 9:2).

The New Testament will apply this to Jesus, and it would not be wise to ignore Jesus' own words where He says "I am the Light of the world; he who follows me will not walk in the darkness, but will have the light of life" (John 8:12). So, the Isaiah 9 prophecy begins well, but it finishes even stronger. Notice the splendor of who Messiah will be, and especially that He will be "Mighty God".

For a child will be born to us, a son will be given to us; And the government will rest on His shoulders; And His name will be called Wonderful Counselor, Mighty God, Eternal Father, Prince of Peace. There will be no end to the increase of His government or of peace, On the throne of David and over his kingdom, To establish it and uphold it with justice and righteousness from then on and forevermore. The zeal of the Lord of hosts will accomplish this (Isaiah 9:6-7).

Anyone who denies that Jesus is God should be distressed by this prophecy. It was written 800 years before Jesus came, and it claims the same thing that Christians have claimed for the last 2000 years. Jesus is God. Strangely, there are some who say that Jesus is Savior, but that He is not God. Isaiah 43:11 would have us perish such a thought. "I, even I, am the Lord, and there is no savior besides Me". So, according to Isaiah, the Savior whom God will send will also be God Himself.

Third, while speaking of the nation of Israel being taken away into captivity, the prophet Isaiah said two incredibly profound things. First, she would give birth to a boy before being utterly dispersed. Second, the nation would come back into being on a single day.

Before she travailed, she brought forth; Before her pain came, she gave birth to a boy. Who has heard such a thing? Who has seen such things? Can a land be born in one day? Can a nation be brought forth all at once? As soon as Zion travailed, she also brought forth her sons (Isaiah 66:7-8).

Many of the people of Judah would later be deported to Babylon, but a remnant, maybe a majority remained in the land.

Under Artaxerxes, many of the deportees returned. In AD 70, the Roman Emperor Nero ransacked Jerusalem, destroyed the Temple and much of the city, and dispersed many of the Jews. By AD 135, the Jews were forbidden (by the Emperor Hadrian) to live there at all. The significance of Isaiah's prophecy is two-fold. First, the event that would provide the hinge for the Gregorian Calendar, the birth of Jesus, happened before the Jews fully went into Diaspora. Just as Isaiah had foretold more than 800 years prior to it happening, "Before her pain came, she gave birth to a boy". Jesus was born just in time.

Second, an unprecedented event took place on May 14th, 1948. Although no nation has ever been able to retain its identity outside of its homeland for more than a few generations, the Jewish people did so for nearly 2000 years, and on May 14th, 1948, Isaiah 66:8 was fulfilled: "Who has heard such a thing? Who has seen such things? Can a land be born in a one day? Can a nation be brought forth all at once?" Not only was God able to bring the nation back into existence in a day, He said that He would in this most remarkable Isaiah prophecy. But these three were only primers for one of the greatest in any of the 39 books of the Old Testament.

There are 15 verses in the middle of the last section of the Book of Isaiah that are absolutely astonishing. Recall that the Great Isaiah Scroll was found in the Dead Sea Scrolls, and it predates the death of Jesus Christ in AD 33. Not only so, the Hebrew Bible had been translated into Greek (the Septuagint) and into other languages (such as the Targums) long before Jesus was born. So no scholar in the world could argue that Isaiah 52:13-53:12 was written after the time of Jesus. It is indisputably prior to Jesus, yet each one of the 15 verses speaks about Him as if Isaiah were watching His suffering unfold! Each verse is worthy of comment.

Behold, my servant will prosper, He will be high and lifted up and greatly exalted (Isaiah 52:13).

Jesus was welcomed like a King when He entered Jerusalem. A week later, the people would turn against Him, since He did not bring an earthly kingdom. But after His return, "He will be high and lifted up and greatly exalted" forever.

Just as many were astonished at you, My people, so His appearance was marred more than any man and His form more than the sons of men (Isaiah 52:14).

Juxtaposed to the opening verse about exaltation comes this verse about humiliation. Jesus is the exalted King. But He came first as a servant. Having come to His own, His own did not receive Him. The Jewish leaders requested that He be crucified, but capital punishment required the Romans. After the Roman soldiers had their way with Him, Jesus was hardly recognizable. Thorns had married His brow. His face had been pummeled and was swollen and stained red.

Thus He will sprinkle many nations, Kings will shut their mouths on account of Him; For what had not been told them they will see, and what they had not heard they will understand (Isaiah 52:15).

On every nation on the planet today, there are men, women, and children who have been sprinkled by the blood of Jesus. We may not have been physically touched by it, but we entered into covenant (Numbers 24) with Jesus when we placed our faith in Him. In so doing, the New Testament explains that we have come "to Jesus, the mediator of a new covenant, and to the sprinkled blood" (Hebrews 12:24).

Who has believed our message? And to whom has the arm of the Lord been revealed? (Isaiah 53:1)

The historical death and resurrection of Jesus is now the primary proposition of a unique message. We call that message "the Gospel", and it is the ambition of every Christian on Planet Earth to share it. It is a message that must be revealed by God, because man in his human reasoning could never arrive at it simply by observing nature and exercising his mental faculties. God's plan, stated here, was to send us—simple messengers—to deliver His good news. Who will believe?

For He grew up before Him like a tender shoot, and like a root out of parched ground; He has no stately form or majesty that we should look upon Him, nor appearance that we should be attracted to Him (Isaiah 53:2).

Not like a powerful angel descending on a ladder from heaven, but like a helpless baby laid in the animals' feeding trough, Jesus came into the world. He grew up the son of a carpenter in the peasant village of Nazareth. Contrary to the depictions of Him painted in the Middle Ages or later, He was not a handsome man with flowing long hair. His appearance was ordinary at best. It was the majesty of who He is and the significance of the work He did on the cross that has attracted the world to Him.

He was despised and forsaken of men, a man of sorrows and acquainted with grief; and like one from whom men hide their face He was despised, and we did not esteem Him (Isaiah 53:3).

After the crowds deserted Him, Jesus looked to His twelve disciples saying, "You do not want to go away also, do you?" (John 6:67). Even they fell asleep when He needed them to pray for Him the night before He had to go to the cross. The following day, He was despised and forsaken like no other who has ever lived. Of all men who deserved esteem, He was the greatest. But what sorrow and grief He tasted from those who should have loved Him.

Surely our griefs He Himself bore, and our sorrows He carried; Yet we ourselves esteemed Him stricken, smitten of God, and afflicted (Isaiah 53:4).

Here is the very heart of the good news. This is precisely what Christians believe about Jesus. This is what one must understand in order to be a Christian. Jesus was our substitute. He bore our punishment in His body. It was not that He ever sinned in any way, but that we each sinned in many ways. He was innocent, but the only innocent One willingly took the sin of the world upon His shoulders. He carried the just desserts of our sins, while the world considers Him stricken and smitten of God.

But He was pierced through for our transgressions, He was crushed for our iniquities; The chastening for our well-being fell upon Him, and by His scourging we are healed (Isaiah 53:5).

The meaning of Jesus' atoning death is once-again shown to be *substitution.* The righteous gives His body to be crushed for the unrighteous. The Sinless One stands in for sinners. And notice by what means the penalty is delivered. There is a scourging, which Jesus did in fact undergo. Pilate presented Him to the people after brutally scourging Him in order to assuage their blood-thirstiness. "Behold the man!" (John 19:5) But they still demanded crucifixion. That being the case, the rest of the prophetic verse in Isaiah was fulfilled. "But He was pierced" with nails through his hands and feet and with a spear through His side.

All of us like sheep have gone astray, each of us has turned to his own way; But the Lord has caused the iniquity of us all to fall on Him (Isaiah 53:6).

Here the idea of substitution begins to be equated to that of lambs, like the Passover Lamb or the lambs that were sacrificed by the High Priest on the Day of Atonement. All people are like lambs in that we wander off from where we belong. Not only do we drift, we rebelliously turn from God in order to go our own way. But Jesus is an obedient lamb who never strayed, even in the thoughts and motivations of His heart.

He was oppressed and He was afflicted, yet He did not open His mouth; Like a Lamb that is led to slaughter, and like a sheep that is silent before its shearers, So He did not open His mouth (Isaiah 53:7).

The Roman Governor Pontius Pilate marveled at Jesus. "You do not speak to me? Do you not know that I have authority to release you and I have authority to crucify you?" (John 19:10). But Jesus offered no defense. He made no appeals. He didn't cry for justice. He could have called angels to defend Him, but no one was taking His life by force. He was giving it willingly.

By oppression and judgment He was taken away; And as for His generation, who considered that He was cut off out of the land of the living for the transgression of my people, to whom the stroke was due? (Isaiah 53:8)

Two things are undeniable from this passage. First, the one spoken about would die. What else could "cut off from the land of the living" mean? Second, He would die vicariously. He would die, but not for His own transgressions. The death stroke was owed to sinful people, but it was not given to those to whom it was due. It fell upon the Lamb who went silently to the slaughter.

His grave was assigned with wicked men, yet He was with a rich man in His death, because He had done no violence, nor was there any deceit in His mouth (Isaiah 53:9).

When Jesus died on the cross, common criminals were crucified to His right and to His left. Crucifixion was the death sentence for wicked men. But Jesus was buried in a rich man's tomb. Joseph of Arimathea had purchased a new tomb that was carved in rock. It would have been very expensive. Jesus only borrowed it until the third day. Consider this one verse alone. Who else can you think of who was executed as a criminal and alongside of criminals, but buried in a rich man's tomb? Is it mere coincidence that Jesus was?

But the Lord was pleased to crush Him, putting Him to grief; If He would render himself as a guilt offering, He will see His offspring, He will prolong His days, and the good pleasure of the Lord will prosper in His hand (Isaiah 53:10).

Who killed Jesus Christ? Some say the Romans. Some say the Jews. Some say you and I. Each of these is correct. But more precisely, it was God the Father who gave Him as a sacrifice. "For God so loved the world that He gave His one and only Son . . ."

(John 3:16). It pleased the Father to crush Him, because the death of Jesus would mean the salvation of all who would believe in Him.

And having accomplished this redemption, Jesus will see His offspring. This does not refer to physical descendants as some blasphemous books allege. It refers to those of us who are born again through faith in Him. When the prophet Isaiah said, "He will prolong His days", he was referring to Jesus' resurrection and subsequent days on earth. All the good pleasure of God is now in the control of the One who was crushed for the Father's pleasure.

As a result of the anguish of His soul, he will see it and be satisfied; By His knowledge the righteous One, My servant, will justify the many, as He will bear their iniquities (Isaiah 53:11).

The death of Jesus satisfied the wrath of God against sin. Those who know this—not just intellectually, but trusting that it avails for them—are considered just in God's sight. "But now apart from the Law the righteousness of God has been manifested, being witnessed by the Law and the Prophets" (Romans 3:21). Isaiah is one such prophet who told about how sinful men can be justified before a Holy God. "But to the one who does not work, but believes in Him who justified the ungodly, his faith is credited as righteousness, just as David also speaks of the blessing on the man to whom God credits righteousness apart from works: Blessed are those whose lawless deeds have been forgiven, and whose sins have been covered. Blessed is the man whose sin the Lord will not take into account" (Romans 4:5-8).

Therefore I will allot Him a portion with the great, and He will divide the booty with the strong; because He poured out Himself to death, and was numbered with the transgressors; Yet He Himself bore the sin of many, and interceded for the transgressors (Isaiah 53:12).

Like a warrior who wins booty from his victory and divides it with his friends, so the Lord Jesus suffered death, but in so doing won the victory and won eternal life for His friends.

The suffering servant prophecy of Isaiah 52:13-53:12 asks a question about to whom the message of the Lord will go. By the end of it, the message has gone out to the many. The arm of the Lord is revealed to you also. Jesus was numbered with the transgressors even though He never transgressed God's Law. You and I have transgressed. But God in His mercy has laid our sin upon the shoulders of Jesus. Jesus served us in this way. He is the suffering servant who came as a baby, grew in obscurity, stood silent like a Lamb, received scourging and piercings, was cut off from the land of the living, yet prolonged His days.

The prophecies of Isaiah are profound. In 7:14 we are told that God will give a sign: "a virgin will be with child and bear a son". In 9:6 we are told "a child born . . . a son given . . . will be called . . . Mighty God, Eternal Father . . ." In 43:11 we learn that there is no Savior but Yahweh. In 66:7-8 the Boy is born before complete Diaspora, and yet the nation will be born in a day. Jesus came at the turn of the Gregorian Calendar before Rome expelled the Jews. Nearly two thousand years later, the nation of Israel was born in a day—May 14, 1948!

In 52:13-53:12 we see details like Jesus standing silent before

Pilate, being scourged, His crucifixion with the wicked, being pierced, His burial in a rich man's tomb, and His resurrection after being cut off from the land of the living. All of these prophecies are God's grace to us. They are the revealing of His arm to us. It is not God's will that we would die in our sins. It is also not required of us that we have blind faith. Rather, He desires for us to place our faith in His Word—to believe in Jesus, the Lamb given to be slaughtered, the suffering servant who was crushed for our iniquities.

CHAPTER 24

SEEN IN THE NEW COVENANT
JEREMIAH

Jeremiah was sent to call Judah to repentance. He did so from 626 BCE right up until the fall of Jerusalem in 586 BCE. For forty years, Jeremiah was a faithful preacher. But for forty years, the people rejected his message. He warned of the coming judgment, but the people (especially the leaders) preferred the message of peace and prosperity foretold by the false prophets. So Jeremiah was often persecuted, even kept in the stocks. But Jeremiah was not a prophet of doom, and had the people repented, they could have averted God's discipline.

Even when it was too late, God didn't send the Jews into Babylonian captivity in order to destroy them, but to correct them. After seventy years of discipline, they would go back to the Promised Land. Jeremiah foretold this. "For thus says the Lord, 'When seventy years have been completed for Babylon, I will visit you and fulfill my good word to you, to bring you back to this place" (Jeremiah 29:10). By no coincidence, the Babylonian captivity did in fact last seventy years. But there was a still greater freedom, a more perfect peace, a spiritual prosperity that awaited the people of God, and Jeremiah foretold this too. God would never abandon His people. He corrects us in order to make us obedient. He even changes the hearts of His people.

Under the Old Covenant, the people were constantly unfaithful. God was faithful to the agreement, but the people were not. It became apparent, especially after Jeremiah prophesied to no avail, that the people were incapable of obeying. The Law, which was given through Moses, was good. But the hearts of the people were not. Ever since the Garden of Eden, sin was a part of human nature. The Law was effective in revealing where the people fell short. It was like a mirror that gave evidence that the hearts of the people were not consistent with the heart of God. So the Old Covenant was necessary to show our need for a Savior, but something more was necessary to actually save us.

"Behold, days are coming," declares the Lord, "when I will make a new covenant with the house of Israel and with the house of Judah, not like the covenant which I made with their fathers in the day I took them by the hand to bring them out of the land of Egypt, My covenant which they broke, although I was a husband to them," declares the Lord. "But this is the covenant which I will make with the house of Israel after those days," declares the Lord, "I will put my law within them and on their heart I will write it; and I will be their God, and they shall be My people. They will not teach again, each man his neighbor and

each man his brother, saying, 'Know the Lord,' for they will all know Me, from the least of them to the greatest of them," declares the Lord, "for I will forgive their iniquity, and their sin I will remember no more" (Jeremiah 31:31-34).

The New Covenant accomplished what the Old could not, because the blood of Jesus was able to accomplish what external laws and regulations could not. The blood of Jesus was truly able to take away sin. The blood of lambs was only a placeholder that pointed to Jesus until He came and died. Once His blood had actually been shed upon the cross, a greater freedom became available.

When the hour had come, He reclined at the table, and the apostles with Him. And He said to them, "I have earnestly desired to eat this Passover with you before I suffer; for I say to you, I shall never again eat it until it is fulfilled in the kingdom of God." And when He had taken a cup and given thanks, He said, "Take this and share it among yourselves; for I say to you, I will not drink of the fruit of the vine from now on until the kingdom of God comes." And when He had taken some bread and given thanks, He broke it and gave it to them, saying, "This is My body which is given for you; do this in remembrance of Me." And in the same way He took the cup after they had eaten, saying, "This cup which is poured out for you is the new covenant in my blood" (Luke 22:14-20).

Something radical happened when the blood of Jesus was poured out on the cross. The Old Covenant gave way to the New. Jesus' blood provided for the forgiveness of sin. From that moment on, when someone believes in Jesus, "their sin I will remember no more" (Jeremiah 31:34). As Jesus mentioned, the Passover Celebration that had been celebrated in Israel for 1500 years brought them to this day. Everything in the Old Covenant was being fulfilled.

The 39 books of Scripture that had been complete (written and preserved) for more than 400 years already were now fully complete. They were not abolished, but fulfilled. So what difference did the New Covenant in Jesus' blood make in the lives of actual people?

It made all the difference because the sins of people were now truly taken away. Prior to this, sins were only covered over. Now they were removed entirely, hence "their sin I will remember no more". It also meant that Gentiles were allowed to share equally in this forgiveness alongside of Israel. When Jesus said, "I shall never again eat it until it is fulfilled in the kingdom of God", He indicated that the shedding of His blood and the initiation of the New Covenant brought the kingdom of God to earth in a new way. After rising from the dead, Jesus told His apostles that the forgiveness of sin provided by the New Covenant is offered to all nations.

He said to them, "Thus it is written, that the Christ would suffer and rise again from the dead the third day, and that repentance for forgiveness of sin would be proclaimed in His name to all nations, beginning from Jerusalem" (Luke 24:46-47).

So, "all nations" are included in the New Covenant. Finally, it meant a radical change of heart for the people of God. Remember that Jeremiah preached for forty years to a constantly disobedient people. They had the Law of Moses to guide their behavior, but they could never live up to it. Jeremiah foresaw a new agreement. "I will put my law within them and on their heart I will write it; and I will be their God, and they shall be My people". This new agreement meant that the price of sin had been paid once and for all. When Jesus died,

He said "it is finished" (John 19:30). Since Jesus accomplished all the work that is required to save people from sin, there is no work left for people to do. There is no room left for people to boast about their own righteousness. There is no amount of religious effort that can add anything to what He accomplished.

What we are left with is the ability to truly worship God from a heart of gratitude. Knowing God is no longer a matter of trying to perform well enough, but constantly falling short. Knowing God becomes a matter of accepting His forgiveness. Genuine worship rises from the heart of a man or woman who knows Who God is and what God has done for him or her. When a believer knows that all of his or her sins are completely forgiven (past, present, and future), he or she is truly free. Worship is in no way compelled by outside rules and regulations. Worship flows from the heart of him who has nothing to offer God but his thanksgiving. We don't bring the blood of a lamb, because God provided that for us. Worship comes from the heart under the New Covenant.

God also does something to the human heart when an individual places his or her faith in Jesus Christ. "And behold, I am sending forth the promise of My Father upon you; but you are to stay in the city until you are clothed with power from on high" (Luke 24:49). Jesus said that He would send forth His Holy Spirit to live inside the hearts of His followers. Therefore He supplies the power that is necessary for believers to truly worship and love God from the heart. The Holy Spirit came during the Jewish Festival of Pentecost. His coming was likened to a great wind and to flames of fire that rested over the heads of the believers and then entered into them. When the Holy Spirit came into them, they received newfound power to worship God from the heart and to witness to the reality of Jesus' death and resurrection.

How is it that 11 of the 12 disciples (the traitor Judas excepted) preached faithfully until the end, even at the cost of their own lives? The answer is the New Covenant. The Holy Spirit lived inside of them and empowered them to witness. They were motivated by love and gratitude to Jesus Christ for the price He paid on their behalf. They worshipped from the heart. When asked to recant their testimony or face a torturous death, they gladly accepted the latter.

Compare that with the generation to whom Jeremiah preached. Although God was a faithful husband to them, they constantly turned away from Him. But Jeremiah foretold the New Covenant, initiated by the blood of Jesus. Peter chose to be crucified upside down because his heart was ablaze for his God. John was tortured many times, even boiled in oil, but his love for God could not be silenced. Each of the others died as martyrs, because they saw the resurrected Jesus and because He gave them the Promise of the Father—the Holy Spirit—and He changed their hearts. This is what the New Covenant brought, just as the Book of Jeremiah promised.

CHAPTER 25

SEEN IN THE WEEPING PROPHET

LAMENTATIONS

After Jeremiah preaches faithfully for 40 years, and for 40 years the people reject his warnings, God allows Babylon to overrun Jerusalem. Jeremiah survives the ordeal and lives to write a lament over the desolated city. The poem is carefully constructed. There are 5 chapters. All but the middle have 22 verses. The one in the middle, the third, has 66 verses. Except for the last chapter, each one is written as an acrostic. The first verse begins with the first letter of the Hebrew alphabet. The second verse begins with the second letter, and so it goes through the 22 letters of the alphabet. In the case of the middle chapter, the 66 verses, each letter begins a three-verse section of Scripture. So, the middle chapter is a crescendo, and it is here that Jesus Christ comes into the sharpest focus. But the entire content of Jeremiah's lament points to Jesus.

The Book of Jeremiah is the agonized cry of the prophet. Some of his descriptions of the destruction of Jerusalem are difficult to read, even for those of us who have been desensitized by what we see on TV. Jeremiah also makes note of his own emotion as he looks on.

My eyes fail because of tears, My spirit is greatly troubled; My heart is poured out on the earth because of the destruction of the daughter of my people, when little ones and infants faint in the streets of the city (Lamentations 2:11).

Jeremiah came to Jerusalem to preach, but 40 years later lamented her fall. Jesus came to the rebuilt Jerusalem, and 40 years later she fell again. Like Jeremiah, Jesus was a prophet. He announced the destruction of Jerusalem before it happened. Jesus ministered between 30 and 33 AD. His words were recorded in the Book of Luke before 55 AD. So historians should acknowledge that Jesus foretold the fall of Jerusalem, just as they acknowledge the actual event that occurred in 70 AD at the hands of the Roman Emperor Nero. Jerusalem fell as Jesus predicted.

When He approached Jerusalem, He saw the city and wept over it, saying, "If you had known in this day, even you, the things which make for peace! But now they have been hidden from your eyes. For the days will come upon you when your enemies will throw up a barricade against you, and surround you and hem you in on every side, and they will level you to the ground and your children within you, and they will not leave in you one stone upon another, because you did not recognize the time of your visitation" (Luke 19:41-44).

Jesus' prophecy was fulfilled in 70 AD. But also notice the emotion of the Lord. He is the weeping prophet that Jeremiah prefigured. When Jesus approached Jerusalem, "He saw the city and wept over it". It was not uncommon for Jesus to weep. "In the days of His flesh, He offered up both prayers and supplications with loud crying and tears" (Hebrews 5:7). It is evident that Jesus does not delight in the destruction of the wicked. Every day, millions of people die and enter into eternity without having repented of their sins or believed in Jesus Christ. Jesus tells us that these people "will be cast out into the outer darkness" (Matthew 8:12) "into the eternal fire which has been prepared for the devil and his angels" (Matthew 25:41). Although Jesus is the Judge who executes this judgment on the wicked, He does not delight in their everlasting punishment. He weeps over them.

But He is especially grieved by the suffering of the innocent on account of the wickedness of others. Jeremiah makes special note of children who suffer through no fault of their own. Their mothers, who should have protected them, have turned against them. Jeremiah weeps uncontrollably as he observes the terrible pain that the sin of others brings upon the children. Similarly, Jeremiah himself was a preacher of righteousness who called for repentance, and yet he also suffered when Jerusalem was destroyed. Lamentations 3 is the crescendo of the book. Each letter of the alphabet receives three verses of lament, rather than one. In this chapter, Jeremiah becomes a type of the innocent suffering of Jesus Christ on behalf of others.

I am the man who has seen affliction because of the rod of His wrath . . . Surely against me He has turned His hand repeatedly all the day . . . Even when I cry out and call for help, He shuts out my prayer . . . I have become a laughingstock to all my people, their mocking song all the day . . . My eyes run down with streams of water because of the destruction of the daughter of my people. My eyes pour down unceasingly, without stopping, until the Lord looks down and sees from heaven. My eyes bring pain to my soul because of all the daughters of my city (Lamentations 3).

Jeremiah was not aloof to the suffering of Jerusalem, although he warned them of it. Rather, he participated in it. And in the most profound way, so did Jesus Christ. Not only did He observe the suffering of the people He loves (including children) and grieve for them, He actually took the physical pain into His own body. He suffered a torturous death in order to remove the penalty of eternal suffering from those who will believe in Him. After being cut off from the land of the living and laid in a tomb, His life was redeemed from the pit. Jeremiah also foreshadowed this resurrection in Lamentations 3 when he remembered to put his hope in the Lord.

My enemies without cause hunted me down like a bird; They have silenced me in the pit and placed a stone on me. Waters flowed from my head; I said, "I am cut off!" I called on your name, O Lord, out of the lowest pit. You have heard my voice, "Do not hide your ear from my prayer for relief, from my cry for help." You drew near me when I called on You; You said, "Do not fear!" O Lord you have pleaded my soul's cause; you have redeemed my life (Lamentations 3:52-58).

Jeremiah was ultimately just another man whom the Lord Jesus redeemed by His own blood. But his experience of being kept like a bird in a cage, his time in a pit with a stone overhead, prefigured the burial of Jesus Christ in a tomb and His victorious resurrection from there. Although the innocent Son of God was forsaken for a time as He died upon a cross, that period of time served the purpose of redeeming the lives of men. Having accomplished this, the Father did not abandon His Son to the grave, but raised Him up from the pit.

Jesus is the weeping prophet. He grieves the destruction of sinners, finding no delight in their death. Even more so, He grieves the suffering of those who are hurt by the sins of others. But His condescension to us is even more personal than that. He took the suffering of the world upon Himself. He died the death that we deserve. Having conquered the grave, He now offers to redeem lives from the pit. Whosoever will call upon His name for salvation will be saved.

CHAPTER 26

SEEN IN THE GLORY OF THE LORD
EZEKIEL

Ezekiel is the most symbolic of the Old Testament books. The author often describes his visions, and many of these pertain to things that are still in the future. In this way, the Book of Ezekiel is a lot like the Book of Revelation in the New Testament. Ezekiel 37 is a vision of a valley of dry bones. The bones come together, receive new ligaments and flesh, and come back to life. Ezekiel tells us that this refers to the whole house of Israel coming back as if from the dead.

When Ezekiel was writing, Israel was in captivity in Babylon and then Persia. But their captivity, beginning in 586 BCE, lasted only 70 years. At that time, they were free to return. But, interestingly, they never became a sovereign nation again, not the way they were before the captivity, that is, until 1948. As unbelievable as it is, on May 14th, 1948 (also in accordance with the Isaiah 66 prophecy), the dry bones once again became animated flesh and bone! Israel is a sovereign nation again. Ezekiel 38 and following chapters describe events that we may one day see unfold before our very eyes. All of this relates to the Second Coming of the Lord Jesus, which hopefully will happen soon. But Ezekiel pointed us to at least one event of Jesus' first appearing.

When Israel completed the first Temple—Solomon's—the glory of the Lord filled it in a special way. It was like a heavy cloud. When Solomon dedicated the Temple to the Lord, the cloud was so thick that the priests couldn't even perform their duties. The celebration on that day was wonderful. In the presence of God, the people ended up lying with their faces to the ground in reverence. We are told that their hearts were also filled with joy.

But years had passed since that day, and generations of increasingly wicked kings had led Israel and Judah further into sin. Demonstrating God's great patience, the Shekinah Glory never departed from the Temple during this time. It was not a thick cloud as on the day of dedication, but the presence of God was in the Holy of Holies in a very special way. Even when the people sinned, they could turn to the Temple and plead for mercy. They would find it there at the Mercy Seat. But something changed during the last days before the fall of the Temple in Ezekiel's day.

Then the glory of the God of Israel went up from the cherub on which it had been, to the threshold of the temple (Ezekiel 9:3) . . . Then the glory of the Lord departed from the threshold of the temple and stood over the cherubim. When the cherubim departed, they lifted their wings and rose up from the earth in my sight with the wheels beside them; and they stood still at the entrance of the east gate of the Lord's house, and the glory of the God of Israel hovered over them (Ezekiel 10:18-19) . . . The glory of the Lord went up from the midst of the city and stood over the mountain which is east of the city (Ezekiel 11:23).

The glory of God remained in the Holy of Holies while Israel drifted further and further into apostasy. Many generations later, the Israelites didn't even recognize that the glory of the Lord was real. They worshipped the gods of the nations, or they simply served themselves. But Ezekiel had eyes to see the spiritual realities that people ignored. He saw this fascinating thing. The glory of the Lord always sat between the two carved cherubim over the Mercy Seat, which covered the Ark of the Covenant. But Ezekiel saw it rise and move to the very edge of the Temple. Sometime later, it moved again and hovered over actual angels whom Ezekiel was able to see. As they moved, so did the glory of the Lord, until it stood still at the entrance of the East Gate. It had left the Temple and was now on the verge of leaving the city of Jerusalem. Later, Ezekiel saw that it actually did leave the city, departing to the mountain that is east of the city. So in various stages, Ezekiel saw the glory of the Lord depart from the Holy of Holies to the threshold of the Temple to the East Gate of Jerusalem to the mountain east of the city.

The Sunday before Jesus was rejected and crucified, He came to the City of Jerusalem and was presented to the people as their King. During this event—what has become known as the Triumphal Entry—the people welcomed Him. The records show that multitudes gathered. They shouted, "Hosanna to the Son of David" (Matthew 21:9). They understood the Davidic Covenant of 2 Samuel 7, so they were welcoming Jesus as King. That is why "most of the crowd spread their coats on the road" (Matthew 21:8) or cut palm branches to wave and lay before Him. They were ready to coronate Him as King.

Of course, days later, when they saw Jesus beaten to within an inch of His life, and thus offering no deliverance from the oppressive Roman Empire, they turned against Him and they all shouted "crucify Him!" (Matthew 27:22). They didn't understand that at His first appearing, the King came to deliver them from the penalty of sin by becoming a sin offering on their behalf. At His second coming, He will establish His rule on earth. And even as they missed the glory of the Lord departing during the days of Ezekiel, they missed the Glory returning to Jerusalem!

When they had approached Jerusalem and had come to Bethpage, at the Mount of Olives . . . the crowds were saying, "This is the prophet Jesus, from Nazareth in Galilee" . . . And Jesus entered the temple and drove out all those who were buying and selling in the temple, and overturned the tables of the money changers and the seats of those who were selling doves. And He said to them, "It is written, 'My House shall be called a House of Prayer', but you are making it a robbers' den." And the blind and the lame came to Him in the temple, and He healed them (Matthew 21:1-14).

The glory of the Lord departed during Ezekiel's day, but Jesus brought it back the same way it left. When Jesus made His Triumphal Entry, He descended from the Mount of Olives, east of the city, entered Jerusalem through the Eastern Gate, went directly into the Temple and filled it with the glory of the Lord! Jesus *is* the Glory of the Lord. When His body entered, the Temple had more glory in it than it did during Solomon's Dedication. Although the people had made it a Robbers' Den, Jesus cleansed the Temple. The subsequent destruction of His body cleansed us from our sins. The presence of the glory of the Lord in the Temple was what made the Temple glorious. Once Jesus was rejected, taken outside to be crucified, there was nothing left to do but tear the Temple down too. That is precisely what happened, just as Jesus predicted just days before His death.

Jesus came out from the temple and was going away when His disciples came up to point out the temple buildings to Him. And He said to them, "Do you not see all these things? Truly I say to you, not one stone here will be left upon another, which will not be torn down" (Matthew 24:1-2).

Jesus' words came true. The Temple was torn down in 70 AD. But not before it fulfilled its purpose, which was to host the presence of the glory of the Lord. As Ezekiel saw it depart from the Holiest Place to the Threshold to the East Gate to the Eastern Mountain, so Jesus Himself descended from the Eastern Mountain through the East Gate past the Threshold and into the Temple to be the Holy of Holies. Jesus is "the image of the invisible God" (Colossians 1:15). He healed blind people in the Temple when He made His Triumphal Entry, and He is still able to heal our blind eyes.

Will you be like the people of Israel who were unable to see the glory of the Lord departing? Or will you come to Jesus—the Glory of the Lord—and ask Him to open your eyes to see Him for who He is. He returned to heaven from that mountain east of Jerusalem. When

He returns, His foot will split it (Zechariah 14:4). So recognize Him now, while there is still time and while there is still room for you at the Mercy Seat.

Jesus Himself is the Glory of the Lord. Jesus said, "Behold, I stand at the door and knock; if anyone hears My voice and opens the door, I will come into him and will dine with him, and he with me" (Revelation 3:20). The events of Revelation will soon unfold, even as Ezekiel foresaw, but it is not too late to open your heart to the Lord. He will make you His temple and fill you with His presence. "But as many as received Him, to them He gave the right to become children of God, even to those who believe in His name" (John 1:12). Will you invite the Lord Jesus—the Glory of God—to come into your life?

CHAPTER 27

SEEN IN THE MESSIAH
DANIEL

Faith in Jesus Christ is not blind. Rather than taking a leap of faith into a random set of beliefs, God commands us to take Him at His Word. When someone tells me that a faith claim is true, I will want to know "according to whom?" Who says that Muhammad is a prophet or Buddha is enlightened? Who says that Joseph Smith got his Book of Mormon from an angel? Why should I trust what someone else says when I wasn't there?

There is nothing wrong with this kind of skepticism. For how could Jesus and Muhammad both be prophets when Jesus said that He would be crucified (Luke 24:7) and Muhammad said that Jesus was never crucified (Surah 4:157)? Surely we should not listen to everyone who claims to be a prophet. But faith in Jesus is a matter of listening to God. While we must not listen to contradictory voices, God gave 39 books of prophetic testimony prior to sending Jesus, who ties it all together. In so doing, the testimony is proven to be from God, not man. "Now He (Jesus) said to them, 'These are My words which I spoke to you while I was still with you, that all things which are written about Me in the Law of Moses and the Prophets and the Psalms must be fulfilled" (Luke 24:44).

The 22 descriptions of the forsaken and crucified Jesus that are found in Psalm 22 prove that Jesus spoke the truth. The descriptions of His death and the meaning of His death found in Isaiah 53 prove the same. These two chapters alone (among the 39 books of testimony) are reason enough to believe in Jesus. And Daniel 9:24-26 provides equally concrete reason to take Jesus at His Word.

Daniel provides a most amazing reason to believe in Jesus. Before we come to it, Daniel has already seen several glimpses of Jesus. When his three friends were thrown into a fiery furnace for refusing to bow down and worship an image of the king of Babylon, the king looked into the furnace and exclaimed, "Look! I see four men loosed and walking about in the midst of the fire without harm, and the appearance of the fourth is like a son of the gods!" (Daniel 9:25). Remember that this is more than 500 years before Christians claimed that the Son of God had come. After protecting the three friends, they emerge unscathed from the flames. Daniel thus recorded that the Son of God saved them. And Daniel also saw another vision of Jesus Christ.

I kept looking until thrones were set up, and the Ancient of Days took His seat; His vesture was like white snow and the hair of His head like pure wool. His throne was ablaze with flames, its wheels were a burning fire . . . I kept looking in the night visions, and behold, with the clouds of heaven One like a Son of Man was coming, and He came up to the Ancient of Days and was presented before Him. And to Him was given dominion, Glory and a kingdom, that all the peoples, nations and men of every language might serve Him. His dominion is an everlasting dominion which will not pass away; and his kingdom is one which will not be destroyed (Daniel 7:9-14).

Daniel's visions are remarkable descriptions of Jesus Christ, given about 500 years before He came. But in order that our faith would be made even more certain, Daniel actually provides the exact date that the Messiah would be presented to Jerusalem and cut off. It is impossible to overstate the significance of this, because the odds of it occurring without divine intervention are infinitesimally small.

Seventy weeks have been decreed for your people and your holy city, to finish the transgression, to make an end of sin, to make atonement for iniquity, to bring in everlasting righteousness, to seal up vision and prophecy and to anoint the most holy place. So you are to know and discern that from the issuing of the decree to restore and rebuild Jerusalem until Messiah the Prince there will be seven weeks and sixty-two weeks; it will be built again, with plaza and moat, even in times of distress. Then after the sixty-two weeks the Messiah will be cut off and have nothing (Daniel 9:24-26).

This prophecy actually gives the precise time when Messiah the Prince will come and be cut off, meaning rejected and killed. Notice that the passage begins with the purpose for which Messiah would be sent. Consistent with the Christian Gospel, it is "to finish transgression, to make an end of sin, to make atonement for iniquity, to bring in everlasting righteousness . . ." So right away the reader's attention should be directed to the only Man in the history of the world who made a credible claim to be able to do these things. He is the Head of the world's largest "religion" and the most famous Man who has ever lived—Jesus Christ. But what truly validates His claim in this passage is that more than 500 years before He came, Daniel gave the precise date of Jesus' Triumphal Entry and National Rejection.

We have given to us 1) a starting point 2) a duration and 3) a conclusion. The prophet exhorts the reader to "know and discern" what they are, so although it will require some historical research and some mathematical analysis, the prophet (who speaks for God) reminds us that the effort is worth it.

The starting point is when the prophetic clock begins ticking. It is "the issuing of the decree to restore and rebuild Jerusalem". The Book of Ezra provides record of the kings of Persia (Cyrus and Darius) giving decrees to restore and rebuild the Temple, but that was for the Temple. King Artaxerxes commissioned Ezra himself to go and rebuild it in 457 BC, but again, that decree was for the rebuilding of the temple. Historians have discovered only one decree to "restore and rebuild Jerusalem". It was the one that King Artaxerxes gave to Nehemiah around Nissan 1, 444 BC, which corresponds on our Gregorian Calendar to March 8, 444 BC. Nehemiah 2:1-8 is an ancient writing that provides this date to historians. The first verse gives the actual date of the event. Verse seven mentions that the decree was put in writing. So it must be considered the starting point for Daniel's prophecy, because no other historical decree matches the criteria of Daniel 9:25, while this one does exactly.

Next, the duration of the prophetic timetable is to be "seven weeks and sixty-two weeks". Easy math tells us that we are talking about 69 weeks, but why is the duration broken into two sections. The first seven weeks refers to how long it will take to actually "restore and rebuild Jerusalem" as the decree of Artaxerxes commissioned Nehemiah to do. The seven weeks will be complete when Jerusalem is "built again, with plaza and moat, even in times of distress". The book of Nehemiah records how Jerusalem was rebuilt, and it did occur under duress (the builders worked with swords strapped to their sides to be ready for attacks).

But how long is a "week", of which we should expect 69? The Hebrews operated off of seven-year cycles. Ground would be farmed for six and lay fallow on the seventh. After seven cycles of seven years, the fiftieth would be celebrated as a great jubilee, and all debts would be forgiven! So, the Jewish people would recognize that a week is *a period of seven years.* Once again, we employ easy math, and we see that the duration is 69 times 7 weeks, or 483 years.

Finally, we have the conclusion of the prophetic timetable. "Then after the sixty-two weeks the Messiah will be cut off and have nothing". So, the first 7 weeks (49 years) will bring about a rebuilt Jerusalem. Sixty-two weeks after that (434 more years) will bring about the Messiah. Not only so, the Messiah will be cut off. Given that the stated purpose of this prophecy was "to finish the transgression, to make an end of sin, to make atonement for iniquity" and given that Christians say that Jesus was rejected by Israel and cut off from the land of the living in order to accomplish precisely this same purpose, wouldn't it be interesting if the rejection of Jesus happened somewhere near 483 years after the starting point of the prophecy?

As it turns out, not only did it happen at a date in the vicinity, it happened on the very day that the prophecy foretold! The Hebrew calendar, which was the one being used when the prophecy was given to Daniel has a 360 day year. So, 483 years on the Jewish calendar is 173,880 days. We use a Gregorian Calendar, which came into being in 1582 AD, and more precisely renders one year to be 365.22 days, so that equates to 476 years and 25 days on our calendar. Starting on March 8, 444 BCE and adding 476 years and 25 days (173,880 days), we arrive at March 29th, 33 AD.

We know that March 29th, 33 AD was the day that Jesus made His Triumphal Entry into Jerusalem, because 5 days later Jesus died during the Passover. Astronomical data and associated tools that calculate the Passover for years gone by will show that the Passover occurred on April 3, 33 AD. So, the concluding date of Daniel's prophecy just so happens to fall on the day that Jesus was presented to Jerusalem as her Messiah, only to be rejected.

The Book of Daniel thus provides a profound reason to believe in Jesus Christ. No other religious figure did anything noteworthy anywhere near the year 33 AD. Buddha (Siddhartha Gautama) was hundreds of years before the time of Christ. Muhammad was more than 600 years after. Joseph Smith died in 1844 AD. But Jesus Christ was validated by the Prophet Daniel. Daniel foresaw a decree to rebuild the desolated city of Jerusalem. God preserved Nehemiah's Book, so chapter 2 verse 1 provided us with the date when this decree actually happened (remember that these things were written half a millennium before Jesus came).

We were told that there would be 173,880 days until "Messiah the Prince" was "cut off". Ancient historians like Josephus and Luke fix the date of Jesus death at April 3rd, 33 AD. Astronomical data relating to the Passover confirms this date. So, it reasonable to conclude that on March 29th, 33 AD Jesus was presented to Israel and "cut off", thus validating His own claim to be "Messiah the Prince". Jesus was rejected as Israel's Messiah on the exact day that Daniel said "Messiah the Prince" would be "cut off".

God did not give Daniel 9:24-26 to make Christians intellectually smug. Rather, He gave such evidence because Jesus came to put an end to sin by making atonement for it. It is His desire that each of us who reads His revelation would believe in the One who was sent to be our Messiah. Only the Messiah can take away our sin. Jesus said, "all the things which are written about Me in the Law of Moses and the Prophets and the Psalms must be fulfilled" (Luke 24:44). The prophecies were written so that we would believe, and so be saved from our sin. "Believe in the Lord Jesus Christ and you will be saved" (Acts 16:31).

CHAPTER 28

SEEN IN THE FAITHFUL ONE

HOSEA

If the Christian Gospel can be described in only one word, then I would say that it is "love". But the direction of that love is what many people misunderstand. Christians make no claim to being better than others. We don't think that we are necessarily better parents, better husbands, or better wives. We don't boast about how loving we are. And if some do, then they miss the point of the Christian Gospel. "In this is love, not that we loved God, but that He loved us and sent His Son to be the propitiation for our sins" (1 John 4:10).

The Christian Gospel is about one-way Love, which only after it has given the ultimate sacrifice, receives any reciprocation at all. Before that sacrifice is made, people can offer words, actions, and emotions that look and sound like love, but it is not genuine and pure. The Book of Hosea reveals the genuine love of the Father, expressed through the selfless gift of the Son, by revealing the inadequacy of the love we offer to God.

Hosea was a faithful husband to his wife Gomer. Sadly, she left him and sold herself as a prostitute. But God told Hosea to go to the market and buy her back out of her harlotry and take her again to be his wife. Although the thought of this was repugnant to any Israelite, the prophet was told to do it, and he obeyed. In so doing, God held him up as an example to Israel. However, contrary to what they wanted to hear, while Hosea was held up as a picture of God's love, Gomer was said to represent Israel.

Then the Lord said to me, "Go again, love a woman who is loved by her husband, yet an adulteress, even as the Lord loves the sons of Israel, though they turn to other gods and love raisin cakes." So I bought her for myself for fifteen shekels of silver and a homer and a half of barley. Then I said to her, "You shall stay with me for many days. You shall not play the harlot, nor shall you have a man; so I will also be toward you." For the sons of Israel will remain for many days without king or prince, without sacrifice or sacred pillar and without ephod or household idols. Afterward the sons of Israel will return and seek the Lord their God and David their king; and they will come trembling to the Lord and to His goodness in the last days (Hosea 3).

As horrible as the image is, we need to understand that all of our sins are a form of spiritual adultery against God. Those who worship idols are forsaking the Maker of heaven and earth in order to worship a thing that man has made out of wood or stone. So it is with us. When we make sports, careers, family, or any other thing in our lives the thing that we most desire, we are turning against our Creator, who made us in His own likeness. When we deliberately disobey our conscience, which He gave us, or any of His written commands, we are being unfaithful to Him. The Book of Hosea helps us to understand that this is the reality. But it also points us to the love of God.

If we are faithless, He remains faithful, for He cannot disown Himself (2 Timothy 2:13).

Even though we have sinned against God, and we are left without king or sacrifice, helplessly offensive to God, yet He still loves us. And His love is not passive. He actively sends His own Son to be like a husband to that group of people who will believe in Him. Jesus is the Son of David and the sacrifice that faithless people like us could not provide for ourselves. God saw us in our most wretched state. "But God demonstrates His own love toward us, in that while we were yet sinners, Christ died for us" (Romans 5:8).

Hosea paid 15 shekels and some barley to buy Gomer's life out of the slave market of sin. God paid the blood of His only Son to rescue us. It totally offends our sense of self-righteousness and even our self-esteem. But the truth that Hosea reveals is that we are adulterous. We have no way back to Him. We stand completely and desperately in need of His mercy. And the good news is that God is just that loving. He loved us and gave His Son as an atoning sacrifice for our sins.

CHAPTER 29

SEEN IN THE BAPTIZER

JOEL

The Book of Joel was the first one to be quoted when Christians first began to preach the Gospel to the world. The reason for this is that Joel prophesied the coming of the Holy Spirit. Jesus clearly told His disciples to wait on preaching about His death and resurrection until after they had received power from heaven. Jesus said, "You are witnesses of these things. And behold, I am sending forth the promise of My Father upon you; but you are to stay in the city until you are clothed with power from on high" (Luke 24:48-49).

The one true God eternally exists in three persons—Father, Son, and Holy Spirit. The Father sent the Son to provide for the forgiveness of sin. After returning to heaven, the Son (and the Father) sent the Holy Spirit to empower believers to preach the message of Jesus Christ to the ends of the earth. So, when Peter first stood up to preach the Gospel, he began with the Book of Joel, because it explained the phenomenon that was connected with the coming of the Holy Spirit.

When the Holy Spirit came to clothe the disciples with power from on high, there were several supernatural occurrences that marked His coming. First, there was the sound of a violent rushing wind inside the house where they were meeting that just came out of nowhere. Next, "there appeared to them tongues as of fire distributing themselves, and they rested on each one of them" (Acts 2:4). Then, the believers began to praise God using a language that they themselves had never learned and did not understand, but people visiting Jerusalem who spoke a great variety of languages heard these believers declaring the wonders of God in their own native language. The series of events was so remarkable that it required an explanation.

The only explanation for the events of this day was that Jesus Christ had baptized His followers with the Holy Spirit. John the Baptist baptized people in a way that might be more familiar to us. He immersed them in water as he called them to repentance and faith. But as John did so, he told of the supernatural and unique way in which Jesus would baptize. Jesus would immerse His followers in the Holy Spirit. "John answered and said to them all, 'As for me, I baptize you with water; but one is coming who is mightier than I, and I am not fit to untie the thong of his sandals; He will baptize you with the Holy Spirit and fire" (Luke 3:16). That Jesus would baptize His disciples with the Holy Spirit and fire is something that both John the Baptist and the Book of Joel prophesied.

It will come about that I will pour out My Spirit on all mankind; and your sons and daughters will prophesy, your old men will dream dreams, your young men will see visions. Even on the male and female servants I will pour out My spirit in those days (Joel 2:28-29).

There is no natural explanation for the fact that the message of the Gospel spread to the entire known world in the first century after Jesus ascended to heaven. The disciples were simple fishermen, a tax collector, and the like. Jesus left them with a very difficult message. Who would believe a story about a Man who is also God who died a criminal's death but rose from the dead? Educated Romans liked wisdom. The Jews wanted signs and wonders. How could a few commoners from the little-known area of Galilee convince the world of what appeared to be a foolish message? The only explanation is that Jesus poured out His Holy Spirit upon them.

The promise of the Book of Joel still applies today. Jesus baptizes His followers with the Holy Spirit and fire. What else could explain what the studies show? Communist China is on course to become the most Christian nation in the world by the year 2030. South Korea and Guatemala currently have among the highest percentage of the population professing faith in Jesus Christ. The Gospel is reaching the most remote places on earth and is even coming full circle back to Jerusalem. The only explanation for the continued progress of the Gospel, penetrating every culture on earth, is that Jesus pours out His Holy Spirit upon His disciples and we bear witness, with power from on high, to the truth about Jesus Christ.

CHAPTER 30

SEEN IN THE DEFENSE OF THE WEAK

AMOS

Sin has devastating effects on every human heart. The Scriptures are clear that unless we are given the gift of salvation, we remain dead in our sin. But the devastating effects of sin are not limited to the individual who sins. People suffer because of illness, natural disasters, accidents or other things that are no fault of their own. These occur because sin is in the world. They were not a part of God's original creation, but when Adam and Eve sinned, death became a reality on the planet.

But the worst form of suffering on earth is that which people inflict upon others. Every kind of injustice occurs on Planet Earth, and for this reason also, God promises to send Jesus. Jesus began His ministry by saying, "The Spirit of the Lord is upon Me, because He anointed Me to preach the Gospel to the poor. He has sent me to proclaim release to the captives, and recovery of sight to the blind, to set free those who are oppressed, to proclaim the favorable year of the Lord" (Luke 4:18-19). When Jesus returns to earth, He will establish His Kingdom of love, justice, and peace on earth. This Kingdom will last forever. Amos looked forward to its coming and pronounced judgment against those who commit injustice on earth.

The Book of Amos speaks a lot about judgment. To those who are the victims of injustice, this comes as good news. God will not stand idly by when the weak fall prey to those who are stronger. God raised up Amos, who was a lowly shepherd, to announce the judgment that God will send upon the oppressors of the weak.

Because they threshed Gilead with implements of sharp iron, so I will send fire . . . Because they deported an entire population to deliver it up to Edom, so I will send fire . . . I will not revoke its punishment, because he pursued his brother with the sword, while he stifled his compassion; his anger also tore continually, and he maintained his fury forever . . . I will not revoke its punishment, because they ripped open the pregnant women of Gilead in order to enlarge their borders . . . I will not revoke its punishment, because they sell the righteous for money and the needy for a pair of sandals. Those who pant after the very dust of the earth on the head of the helpless also turn aside the way of the humble (Amos 1-2).

God cares about the victims of oppression. In the Book of Amos, He announces a list of people whom He will punish for their specific injustices. God will come to the defense of the weak. This also lends expectation that God will one day establish lasting justice throughout Planet Earth. The person to establish God's Kingdom on earth will be Jesus Christ, the Son of David.

"*In that day I will raise up the fallen booth of David . . . the mountains will drip sweet wine and all the hills will be dissolved. And I will restore the captivity of My people Israel, and they will rebuild the ruined cities and live in them; they will also plant vineyards and drink their wine, and make gardens and eat their fruit. I will also plant them on their land, and they will not again be rooted out from their land which I have given them," says the Lord (Amos 9:11-15).*

Jesus is the Son of David and the Son of God, so He is the one to raise up the fallen booth of David. He will establish His Kingdom on earth when He returns to earth. On that day, every innocent captive will be set free. That which sin has ruined will be brought back to how it originally was in the Garden of Eden. The land will once again produce fruit and vegetables as effectively as it did in the garden. What's more, there will be no more oppression or injustice on earth. No one will get uprooted from their land. The just King will sit on His throne. But until that day, Jesus has taught us how we can live in a world that remains full of injustice.

And turning His gaze toward His disciples, He began to say, "Blessed are you who are poor, for yours is the kingdom of God. Blessed are you who hunger now, for you shall be satisfied. Blessed are you who weep now, for you shall laugh. Blessed are you when men hate you, and ostracize you, and insult you, and scorn your name as evil, for the sake of the Son of Man. Be glad in that day and leap for joy, for behold, your reward is great in heaven. For in the same way their fathers used to treat the prophets" (Luke 6:20-23).

Jesus will bring the Kingdom of God, and when He does, the hungry will be satisfied, the weeping will laugh, those who are hated because of their testimony about Jesus Christ will be honored. The prophet Amos spoke out against the injustices he saw, and so he was persecuted, like all the prophets were. But consistent with the teaching of Jesus, Amos ended his book on a joyful and hopeful note. He saw the coming Kingdom of God as the restoration of "the fallen booth of David".

Since Jesus is the Son of David, Amos was looking ahead to the Kingdom that Jesus will bring. Until that time, we can rest assured that God is already on His throne, and the Kingdom of God is soon to be fully revealed. The Book of Amos points us to Jesus, who alone can bring the Kingdom of God. Amos longed for the coming of the Son of David to bring justice, and Jesus Christ is that defender of the weak.

CHAPTER 31

SEEN IN THE BETRAYED

OBADIAH

The Book of Obadiah is only 21 verses long, but it provides one key ingredient to the picture of Jesus Christ that the Old Testament paints. Prophecy is history written before it comes to pass. And truly, the story of Jesus Christ was written at least 400 years before He came, because all of the 39 books were completed by then. Obadiah is no exception, written more than 500 years before Christ. It paints a picture of the son of Jacob betrayed by the son of Esau.

Jacob and Esau were twins whose struggle with one another began when they were still in the womb. As each grew to be men, nations came from their line. God changed Jacob's name to Israel, and his 12 sons begat the 12 tribes of the nation. Esau gave rise to the nation of Edom. As generations passed, these two nations drifted farther and farther apart. Although they shared Abraham and Sarah, Isaac and Rebekah as their common parents and grandparents, they no longer served as their brother's keeper. But the strife came to a climax during the days of Obadiah when a foreign army attacked Israel and Edom stood idly by.

On the day that you stood aloof, on the day that strangers carried off his wealth, and foreigners entered his gate and cast lots for Jerusalem—you too were as one of them (Obadiah 1:11).

As a result of Edom's terrible wickedness, especially when they gloated over the destruction of their own brother Israel, God determined to utterly destroy this nation. God had already distinguished between the two. Before they were even born, God said "the older will serve the younger" (Genesis 25:23). Edom—the firstborn—failed to serve his brother's interest. So the nation itself failed and was consigned to the fate of becoming "as if they had never existed" (Obadiah 1:16).

The betrayal of Jacob by his brother Esau is also part of the story of Jesus Christ. Being the Messiah, Jesus was more than an ordinary Israelite. He was a descendant of Jacob, but more than that, he was the embodiment of what Israel was meant to be. At every point where the nation stumbled, the nation's Christ remained steadfast. Every one of the laws that the nation of Israel broke, the nation's Messiah kept. He was the perfectly obedient Son. Nevertheless, the nation that should have celebrated their Representative rejected Him instead. Judas became the face of this betrayal. He was like a brother to Jesus. He was one of the twelve. He ate with Jesus daily and followed His lead for three years. Yet Judas famously betrayed Jesus with a kiss. The kiss identified Jesus in the dark of night so that the Romans could take Him prisoner.

The sufferings that Jesus endured from that moment on mirror what happened to Israel when they were invaded in the days of Obadiah. God's own Son was ransacked, beaten, humiliated, and exiled. The mighty Empire took Jesus and brought Him before the Roman Governor—Pontius Pilate—to be tried. Pilate saw no fault in the man, but he was under duress to have Jesus crucified. Not knowing what to do, Pilate looked to someone who could have intervened to rescue the oppressed Messiah. Pilate sent him to Herod, who at that time was a rival. But Herod treated Jesus the same way that the Romans did. "You too were as one of them" (Obadiah 1:11). He mocked Jesus and stood idly by as the Romans carried Jesus off to be crucified. Pilate and Herod became friends that day, after treating Jesus the same way. And who was this Herod who stood aloof as strangers carried Jesus away? He was an Edomite!

Herod was one of the last remaining Edomites, and his own destruction was not far off. All of the line of the Herods who ruled as kings over Israel suffered terrible deaths. Acts 12:23 records how intestinal worms led to the death of Herod Agrippa. Obadiah was a book of judgment against Edom, and the reason for their judgment was their mocking indifference toward the destruction of Israel. When Jesus—the son of Jacob—was taken captive, his own brother—the son of Esau—stood aloof and even delighted in Messiah's death.

Do not gloat over your brother's day, the day of his misfortune. And do not rejoice over the sons of Judah in the day of their destruction; Yes, do not boast in the day of their distress (Obadiah 1:12).

Jesus is a son of Jacob and of Judah. Herod was a son of Esau. Herod gloated over the distress of Jesus. Herod appeared to prosper for a time, but he was destined to fall. Jesus appeared to be defeated for a time, but He was destined to rise.

CHAPTER 32

SEEN IN THE RESURRECTED

JONAH

Most people have heard the story of Jonah being swallowed by a great fish and emerging to tell about it. But few understand that the story points to the resurrection of Jesus Christ. Jonah was sent to Nineveh to warn the people about God's coming judgment. But Jonah was so judgmental that he refused to give them the warning. He knew that if the people heeded God's warning and repented, then God would forgive them. Jonah wanted to leave them alone in their sin, so they could reap what they'd sowed. During this time, Jonah serves as an anti-type to the Savior Jesus Christ. Jesus was willing to come to earth to rescue sinners from the penalty of death. But Jonah ran in the opposite direction.

It is interesting to note, however, that Jonah is the author of the book that tells his story. Since in his own autobiography, he casts himself in a bad light and even ends his story with him pouting about the mercy of God, it is clear that Jonah had a change of heart. He uses his own hard-heartedness to call his readers to compassion. He demonstrates the kindness of God by juxtaposing it to his own lack of concern. So, in the writing of the book of Jonah, Jonah reveals the kind of heart that we should expect Messiah to have. Jonah also dies a figurative death, and figuratively speaking, he rises from the dead.

Many people say that they would believe in Jesus if only He would give them a supernatural sign to prove that He is real. In making this demand, they fancy themselves to be God's puppet master. They want God to perform on demand. But what they fail to recognize is that God sets the terms for how He chooses to reveal Himself. And although God may occasionally grant signs and wonders as a token of His grace to help people believe, the primary evidence He has given is the Word of God. If people refuse to believe the written Word (or even read it), then God may leave them in their defiant and demanding sinfulness.

The Pharisees and Sadducees came up, and testing Jesus, they asked Him to show them a sign from heaven. But He replied to them, "When it is evening, you say, 'It will be fair weather, for the sky is red.' And in the morning, 'There will be a storm today, for the sky is red and threatening.' Do you know how to discern the appearance of the sky but cannot discern the signs of the times? An evil and adulterous generation seeks after a sign; and a sign will not be given it, except the sign of Jonah." And He left them and went away (Matthew 16:1-4).

Jesus left them in their sin because they demanded a supernatural sign but they refused to discern what was written in the Scriptures. The "signs of the times" were all the ways that Messiah was fulfilling the prophecies of the Old Testament right before their eyes. Since they were completely missing it, Jesus pointed them to yet one more that was about to come to pass, "the sign of Jonah".

Jonah points us to Jesus Christ by figuratively rising from the dead. Jonah was thrown into the ocean and swallowed by a great fish because of his own sin. In this, he prefigures the death of Jesus, who did not die for his own sin, but for the sin of others, including Jonah. But in the belly of the fish, the world would assume that Jonah was buried forever. Not so. Miraculously, after three days, the fish spit Jonah up on the shore. Jonah figuratively rose from the dead!

Two things are significant here. First, there is the obvious parallel between Jonah returning to the land of the living and Jesus being resurrected from the dead. This is the sign that Jesus wanted the Pharisees and Sadducees to recognize. He also gave this sign for skeptics today. If only they will look humbly at the signposts that are found in each of the 39 books of the Old Testament and compare those with the testimony of the New Testament, then they also will believe in Jesus Christ.

But secondly, there is also Jonah's prayer from the belly of the fish. Jonah was there on account of his own sin, so he needed to be saved. There was absolutely nothing that he could do to save himself. All he could do was believe in the God who is able to save. And so he prayed and modeled the kind of helpless plea that sinners ought to offer God.

I called out of my distress to the Lord, and he answered me. I cried for help from the depth of Sheol; You heard my voice. For you had cast me into the deep, into the heart of the seas, and the current engulfed me. All of your breakers and billows passed over me . . . while I was fainting away, I remembered the Lord, and my prayer came to you . . . salvation is from the Lord (Jonah 2:2-9).

Salvation is from the Lord. Just as God saved Jonah from his helpless state, He will save you and I if we are willing to confess, "salvation is from the Lord". Remember that the name Jesus, from the Hebrew Yehoshu'a literally means "Yahweh is salvation". If you confess with your mouth that Jesus is Yahweh (Jesus is Lord) and believe in your heart that God the Father raised Jesus from the dead, even as Jonah came out from the fish, then like Jonah, you will be saved.

If you have been waiting for God to give you a sign to help you believe, then consider what you are reading. Even now, God is giving you the sign of Jonah. Together with the other 38 books of the Old Testament, it tells about the death and resurrection of Jesus Christ more than 400 years before the event happened. The resurrection of Jesus Christ and the Old Testament are the greatest supernatural signs that God is willing to give. We are on His terms, and He calls us to believe. In His great mercy, He has given these signs, which are reason enough to believe. If God's heart was like Jonah's heart toward Nineveh, then He would have left us in our sin. But He didn't. Jesus came to save us. Don't be like the Pharisees and Sadducees. Stop doubting and believe. Salvation is from the Lord.

CHAPTER 33

SEEN IN THE BETHLEHEM BORN

MICAH

Micah was the book that rescued my faith when it was on the verge of collapse. When I was a college student, liberal professors attacked my belief in the inerrancy of Scripture. They pointed out every place where the Bible seemed to contradict itself. They confronted me with the problem of theodicy. If there exists this all-powerful and all-loving God, then how is there evil in the world?

I was a Religious Studies Minor, and it seemed to me that everyone else in the class was willing to agree with the professors. If my belief in the Bible was founded, then why wasn't anyone else seeing it? Could it be that my parents had it wrong? Could it be that I only believed the things I did because that was the way I was taught? Was there any objective reason to believe that the message of Jesus Christ was true? Was there reason to trust what the Bible says? My faith was wavering.

Late one night, I called out to the Lord. "If this book is really true, please show me," I prayed. Then I let it fall open. I looked down upon the fifth chapter of the Book of Micah. I remembered that Micah wrote his words more than 700 years before Jesus Christ came. Yet there He was, Jesus Christ! As I considered the prophecy, I realized that unless the Bible was truly God's Word, such words could never have been written. If Jesus wasn't truly the Christ, then how is it that He fulfilled even this one prophecy, let alone the hundreds of others that were written long before He came?

Today I know that I could have flipped to any book of the Old Testament and found within those pages objective evidence that Jesus is Messiah. But God directed me to just the place that He knew would convince me. It was all I needed. Imposters can fake a lot of things. But if Jesus was a liar with no conscience, bent on deceiving the world, then how did He control the place of His birth? Friend and foe alike acknowledged that He was born in Bethlehem. Even if someone set out to fulfill the prophecies, how could He control the place of His own birth? That (as well as countless other prophecies) was something that would be beyond an imposter's control. Bethlehem was a tiny village of little significance, except that the prophet Micah recorded history before it came to pass and marked Bethlehem as the place of Messiah's birth.

But as for you, Bethlehem Ephrathah, too little to be among the clans of Judah, from you One will go forth for Me to be ruler in Israel. His goings forth are from long ago, from the days of eternity (Micah 5:2).

Not only are we given the shorthand "Bethlehem" or even an allusion like "the place of David's birth", we are given the full proper name of the city, "Bethlehem Ephrathah". It is as if Micah was being careful that no one would ever confuse the place of his prophecy with any other place on earth. Messiah must be born here. If he is not, then consider him an imposter.

No one but the Lord Jesus Christ could have fulfilled this prophecy. Remember what Jesus said in John 8:58. "Before Abraham was even born, I am". Jesus is a descendant of David, born in the same city as the former king. But there is something that makes Jesus far greater. Not only is He the offspring of David, He is also the Root. Jesus has eternally existed. He is the "I AM", the uncreated, self-sufficient, eternally existent One. Jesus was born in Bethlehem, but He wasn't created there. He wasn't even created at conception. He always existed, but entered Mary's womb in order to be born as a man. In this way, He added humanity to His eternal Deity. Jesus has always existed, but He took on flesh and blood in order to save humans. Micah saw this about the coming Messiah. "His goings forth are from long ago, from the days of eternity".

Micah 5:2 was reason enough for me to continue believing in Jesus Christ when my faith was challenged. It tells the exact location of Messiah's birth more than 700 years before He was born. It also tells that although Messiah will be born, He has always existed and was never created. This is the cardinal message of Christianity. Jesus is the Son of God as well as the Son of Man. He took on flesh in order to die in the place of sinners and rise from the dead. He returned to His Father from whom He came. This is what we believe, and Micah 5:2 reassures us that we do so because it is true, not just because it is what we want to believe. The prophecies are objective reasons to believe in Jesus Christ and the reliability of the Bible. Jesus, not any other so-called "great" religious leader, was Bethlehem born.

CHAPTER 34

SEEN IN THE WRATH SATISFACTION

NAHUM

There is a difficult truth that many Christians do not like to talk about, but we must. It is the wrath of God. The glorious truth of the Gospel is that the love of God has motivated Him to send His one and only Son to receive the wrath of God by becoming a propitiation in the place of sinful people. Since Jesus satisfied the wrath of God, none of it remains for us who belong to Jesus. But the oft-neglected truth that underlies this good news is that God has wrath. So, what does that mean for those who do not belong to Jesus Christ? The Book of Nahum points people to Jesus Christ by demonstrating what will happen to those who reject the salvation that God has made available in Jesus Christ.

The key to understanding the message of Nahum and how it relates to Jesus Christ is in remembering the Book of Jonah. The Assyrians were exceedingly wicked, and Nineveh their capital was a place of extreme violence. As visitors approached the city, they were greeted by the skin of Assyria's victims draped over Nineveh's wall. Even the Babylonians, who were ruthless themselves and who eventually conquered Assyria, were appalled by what they found there. It is understandable why Jonah ran in the opposite direction when God sent him to offer Nineveh the opportunity to repent.

But God did extend an offer of mercy, and by no merit of their own, they accepted the offer and received forgiveness. The city averted God's judgment on account of God's great mercy. So when Nahum speaks to the fate of the city about a hundred years later, it is against the backdrop of what happened through Jonah. Sadly, the people who received the knowledge of Yahweh and should have been His worshipers had returned to their previous idols and even worsened their violent behavior. What then would God do?

A jealous and avenging God is the Lord; the Lord is avenging and wrathful. The Lord takes revenge on His adversaries, and He reserves wrath for His enemies. The Lord is slow to anger and great in power, and the Lord will by no means leave the guilty unpunished. In whirlwind and storm is His way, and clouds are the dust beneath His feet (Nahum 1:2-3).

Many people wrongly say that the God of the Old Testament is a God of wrath while the God of the New Testament is a God of love. There is no such distinction in the Bible. The attributes of God are unchanging, and He displays both His love and His wrath in equal measure in each of the Testaments. Notice in the passage above, "the Lord is slow to anger".

God extended the offer of salvation to the city, but although their repentance was genuine at the time, and perhaps lasted for that generation, the current generation was willfully disobedient to God. They rejected His mercy and received the only thing that was left. The river that fed the moat that surrounded the city ate away at the foundation of the wall. It eventually fell, crushing many, drowning many, and exposing the people to the sword of Babylon. The words of Nahum came to pass. He spoke judgment from beginning to end. And a similar warning is given to those who reject salvation in Christ.

Anyone who has set aside the Law of Moses dies without mercy on the testimony of two or three witnesses. How much severer punishment do you think he will deserve who has trampled underfoot the Son of God, and has regarded as unclean the blood of the covenant by which he was sanctified, and has insulted the Spirit of grace? For we know Him who said, "Vengeance is mine, I will repay." And again, "It is a terrifying thing to fall into the hands of the living God" (Hebrews 10:28-31).

God is slow to anger. He is so loving that He gave His one and only Son to save anyone who is willing to receive Him as Lord and Savior. But if someone rejects the salvation that God offers through Jesus Christ, and he rejects that salvation right through his dying breath, should he expect God to make yet another way for him?

No, the Father regards the blood of Jesus as being too precious to be ignored. There is nothing more gracious than the offer of salvation made available in God's only Son. But if a man rejects even this, then the insult is too great. Nothing but God's wrath remains for such a person. The words of Nahum came true for Nineveh, so we must heed them as well.

There is no relief for your breakdown, your wound is incurable (Nahum 3:19).

The idea of suffering eternally is too much for us to wrap our minds around. But Jesus speaks of hell more than anyone else in the Bible. The reality of an "incurable wound" and "no relief" for all eternity should make us tremble. It is wise to have a healthy fear of God. He is the all-powerful Creator of all. But His perfect love casts out all fear for those of us who believe in Jesus Christ.

The Book of Nahum leads us to Christ because it demonstrates just what it is that Jesus has spared us from. We must understand the wrath of God in order to truly receive His mercy. The Assyrians thought that their wall was too big to ever fall, but it was a leaf in the wind before the breath of God. Our defenses against the wrath of God are the same. No one will be able to talk his way out of God's judgment. No one has a list of good works that will serve as a wall of protection on the Day of Judgment. So fear God and cling to the cross of Jesus Christ while there is still time. The days of your life are a breath away from ending, and God's wrath can flare up in a moment. Flee to take hold of Christ and rest in His promise that you will be saved. Yahweh is salvation, so trust Jesus while there is still time.

CHAPTER 35

SEEN IN THE RIGHTEOUSNESS GIVEN

HABAKKUK

Not everyone who claims to be a Christian is one genuinely. Early in the 16th Century, virtually everyone on the continent of Europe claimed to be Christian, but many were not. The only churches that the people had were Roman Catholic, and many of the leaders were corrupt. In order to fund building projects like St. Peter's Basilica and in order to finance wars like the one against the Turks, the Pope commissioned the practice of selling indulgences. Priests would travel throughout the land selling pieces of paper that promised to release loved ones from the fires of Purgatory. "When a coin in the coffer rings, a soul from Purgatory springs". How the genuine Christians must have cried out to God when they saw such deception.

A young man named Martin Luther had a particularly acute conscience. After nearly dying from a lightning strike, he vowed to become a priest. He began to spend hours confessing his sins every day. The harder he tried to be righteous, the more he sensed his own shortcomings. He constantly felt that he was condemned under the wrath of God. But something happened that opened his eyes to the glorious truth of the Gospel. Once his eyes were opened, he began to share the truth with others, and the Protestant Reformation began. The continent of Europe would never be the same as the eyes of millions of people were opened to the true message of Jesus Christ. The verse that awakened faith in Martin Luther was a New Testament quotation from the Book of Habakkuk.

The default position of our human reasoning is that we will be righteous if we control our behavior to the best of our ability. We think that we can earn God's acceptance if we perform well enough. Martin Luther was scared to death of offending God, so he strove to be pious. But the truth shall set us free. What he learned and what we need to see is that the Lord is our Righteousness. He does not measure our good works against our bad works. He imputes His own righteousness to those who believe in Him. Habakkuk proclaimed this essential truth. Just as it opened Martin Luther's eyes and a million eyes across Europe, it is able to do the same for us.

But the righteous will live by his faith (Habakkuk 2:4).

This verse is as profound as it is short. But it is easy to misunderstand. It does not mean that righteous people will demonstrate their righteousness by how they live. Rather, it means that what makes someone both righteous and spiritually alive is that person's faith. One's faith need only be genuine and placed in the proper object. If a man puts his trust in the sun or the moon, those inanimate objects have no power to credit righteousness to the person. God alone can declare a person righteous. When someone places trust in Jesus Christ, God credits it to that person as righteousness. Regardless of his behavioral track record and regardless of future performance, God considers him righteous who believes in His Son.

The Book of Habakkuk is one of questions, and this honesty is important. The prophet questions God as to why the wicked prosper. The people of Judah have turned against God, yet they get away with it. God answers Habakkuk, telling him that God will soon punish the Israelites with the sword of Babylon. Although this answers the question, it also raises another. "Why are you silent when the wicked swallow up those more righteous than they?" (Habakkuk 2:13) In others words, why would You use an even more wicked nation to bring judgment on Judah? God answers that He will also judge Babylon. In the end, Habakkuk undoubtedly has more questions, and his mind is not set at ease, but he chooses to leave God's secret things to Him and continue to have faith.

I heard and my inward parts trembled, at the sound my lips quivered. Decay enters my bones, and in my place I tremble. Because I must wait quietly for the day of distress, for the people to arise who will invade us. Though the fig tree should not blossom and there be no fruit on the vines, though the yield of the olive should fail, and the fields produce no food, though the flock should be cut off from the fold and there be no cattle in the stalls, yet I will exult in the Lord, I will exult in the God of my salvation (Habakkuk 3:16-18).

Perhaps you have questions that you want God to answer. The Book of Habakkuk gives us permission to ask. God often makes known many things that we didn't know He would answer. "Call to Me and I will answer you, and I will tell you great and mighty things, which you do not know" (Jeremiah 33:3). He is certain to tell us everything that we need to know. But there are also things that He will choose to keep secret from us. And faith requires that we ultimately acquiesce to this. "The secret things belong to the Lord our God, but those things which are revealed belong to us and our children forever" (Deuteronomy 29:29).

Look to Habakkuk as an example of faith. He trembled as he waited for Babylon to invade. Imagine the questions that ran through his mind. But in the midst of uncertainty, he was able to worship the Lord and even rejoice in the God of his salvation. In like manner, can you say that it is enough for you that Jesus Christ died for your sins? Even if you still have questions about the Bible or questions about why things have happened the way they have in your own life, are you willing to believe that God is good, His love is genuine, and He declares you righteous when you put your faith in Jesus? Nothing more need be known or said than what we learned from Habakkuk. But it must be understood the way God revealed it: "The righteous will live by faith".

CHAPTER 36

SEEN IN THE DIVIDER
ZEPHANIAH

Jesus told a parable about an enemy who sowed weeds into his neighbor's field. When it was discovered, the owner determined to let the wheat and the weeds grow up together. The plan was to separate them on the day of the harvest. Jesus told another parable, this time about sheep and goats. They coexist, but on a certain day, they are separated. The sheep enter into heaven, and the goats are sent to hell. In both parables, there is an age when two groups appear to be the same but are awaiting completely opposite destinies. The Book of Zephaniah is about "the Day of the Lord", the same day that Jesus taught about in His parables.

Jesus' parables indicate that there will be an age when believers and unbelievers exist side by side and seem to have similar lives. But in a drastic turn of events, on "the Day of the Lord", they get separated from each other and are treated in exactly opposite ways. Those symbolized by weeds and goats are cast into an eternal fire.

Those symbolized by wheat and sheep are brought into an eternal paradise. The Book of Zephaniah, although it may appear dark at first glance, is a necessary and loving warning to us. It alarms us and keeps us from being lulled into a sleep. If it seems that the righteous and the sinner are treated the same, it is an appearance that will come to a drastic end on the Day of the Lord.

It will come about at that time that I will search Jerusalem with lamps, and I will punish the men who are stagnant in spirit, who say in their hearts, "The Lord will not do good or evil!" Moreover their wealth will become plunder and their houses desolate; Yes, they will build houses but not inhabit them, and plant vineyards but not drink their wine.' Near is the great day of the Lord, near and coming very quickly; Listen, the day of the Lord! In it the warrior cries out bitterly. A day of wrath is that day, a day of trouble and distress, a day of destruction and desolation, a day of darkness and gloom, a day of clouds and thick darkness (Zephaniah 1:12-15).

Many people imagine Jesus to be an almost feminine figure. But the Book of Zephaniah describes the lead-up to Christ's Second Coming and the separation that happens when He comes. The Day of the Lord Jesus will be glorious for believers, but dreadful for the lost.

"Therefore wait for Me," declares the Lord, "for the day when I rise up as a witness. Indeed, My decision is to gather nations, to assemble kingdoms, to pour out on them My indignation, all my burning anger; for all the earth will be devoured by the fire of my zeal. For then I will give to the peoples purified lips, that all of them may call on the name of the Lord, to serve Him shoulder to shoulder . . . For then I will remove from your midst your proud, exulting ones.

And you will never again be haughty on My holy mountain. But I will leave among you a humble and lowly people, and they will take refuge in the name of the Lord. The remnant of Israel will do no wrong and tell no lies, nor will a deceitful tongue be found in their mouths; for they will feed and lie down with no one to make them tremble" (Zephaniah 3:8-13).

Jesus is gentle toward His sheep. He washes us white as snow with His own blood. But He is hard on the goats. He destroys them with fire. Isaiah foretold that "with the breath of his lips He will slay the wicked" (Isaiah 11:4). The Book of Revelation in the New Testament, which pictures the same Day of the Lord that Zephaniah foresaw, describes Jesus this way.

And I saw heaven opened, and behold, a white horse, and He who sat on it is called Faithful and True, and in righteousness He judges and wages war. His eyes are a flame of fire, and on His head are many diadems; and He has a name written on Him which no one knows except Himself. He is clothed with a robe dipped in blood, and His name is called the Word of God (Revelation 19:11-13).

The Day of the Lord Jesus will be one of separation, but we live in an age of coexistence. In the Book of Zephaniah, God told us "Therefore, wait for Me" (Zephaniah 3:8). The New Testament also told us that the apparent status quo would lull many to sleep and cause many to believe that the Day of the Lord is only a figment of Christian imagination.

Know this first of all, that in the last days mockers will come with their mocking, following after their own lusts, and saying, "Where is the promise of His coming? For ever since the fathers fell asleep, all continues just as it was from the beginning of creation." For when they maintain this, it escapes their notice that by the word of God the heavens existed long ago and the earth was formed out of water and by water, through which the world at that time was destroyed, being flooded with water. But by His word the present heavens and earth are being reserved for fire, kept for the day of judgment and destruction of ungodly men. But do not let this one fact escape your notice, beloved, that with the Lord one day is like a thousand years, and a thousand years like a day. The Lord is not slow about His promise, as some count slowness, but is patient toward you, not wishing for any man to perish but for all to come to repentance (2 Peter 3:3-9).

God doesn't desire to destroy anyone on the Day of the Lord. He wants everyone to repent and believe in the Lord Jesus now and wait for His appearing. Those who are waiting will rejoice to see their Lord on that Day. But Zephaniah warns that many will not be ready. They thought that the Lord would never really do anything. They mocked the Christian claim that Jesus is coming back soon. The prophet exposes what terrible folly this is. He calls everyone to repent now, before the Day of the Lord comes upon the world like a flood. Today is the day of salvation.

CHAPTER 37

SEEN IN THE FOUNDATION

HAGGAI

There are two questions that I eventually like to ask people when I meet them. "What are you living for?" and "How is that working?" What I usually find is that unless the person is living for Jesus Christ, they have a sense that life isn't working. They may have enough money. But if they are living for their jobs, they aren't feeling satisfied or experiencing true life through their work. If they are living for their family, they still sense that something is missing. Haggai puts his finger on this experience in an effort to call the people to faith in Yahweh, who is the only satisfaction for the human soul.

Jesus Christ calls Himself "the way, the truth, and the life" (John 14:6). He says that He is "the Resurrection and the Life" (John 11:25). Christians agree and echo the words of Paul, "For to me, to live is Christ and to die is gain" (Philippians 1:21). To really be alive, to feel satisfaction at the core of the human soul, requires faith in the One who is the Author of Life—Jesus Christ. Without Him, life just won't work.

Now therefore, thus says the Lord of hosts, "Consider your ways! You have sown much, but harvest little; you eat, but there is not enough to be satisfied; you drink, but there is not enough to become drunk; you put on clothing, but no one is warm enough; and he who earns, earns wages to put into a purse with holes" (Haggai 1:5-6).

Haggai called the people to consider their ways as part of his prophetic rebuke. The Temple of God remained in ruins as they concerned themselves entirely with their own lives. They were worried about putting paneling on their houses, but the Temple of God was a heap of stones. In response to the call, a leader named Zerubbabel led the people to put their hands to the work of rebuilding the Temple. Zerubbabel is a type of Christ for two reasons. First, he was a direct ancestor of Jesus Christ. His name appears on the first page of the New Testament as Matthew traces out the lineage of Messiah. Second, he laid the foundation of the Temple.

For no man can lay a foundation other than the one which is laid, which is Jesus Christ (1 Corinthians 3:11).

Jesus is the foundation upon which the Church is built. Visit any genuine church on the planet, and His Name will be the subject of the worship and the preaching. He is also the One upon whom individual Christians base our lives. We place all of our hope in Him. If it turned out that He was not real, then we should be pitied more than all men, because we forsake everything else in the world if only to have Him. But Jesus always proves Himself to be a sure foundation. Once the people responded to Haggai's preaching and Zerubbabel led them to lay the foundation for the rebuilt Temple, everything changed for the people.

Do consider from this day onward, from the twenty-fourth day of the ninth month; from the day when the temple of the Lord was founded, consider: Is the seed still in the barn? Even including the vine, the fig tree, the pomegranate and the olive tree, it has not borne fruit. Yet from this day on I will bless you (Haggai 2:18-20).

Once they had the right foundation, life began to make sense. This didn't mean that they would be rich and famous. Rather, it meant that life would "work". Moreover, they would feel truly satisfied. Even though they were no longer living for themselves (no longer paneling their houses), they felt as if they were really living. They had a purpose bigger than themselves to live for. And it wasn't just a random purpose. It was based on the real purpose of the one true God.

What are you living for? Stop and consider what it is that motivates your life, what you think about most when your mind isn't occupied by responsibilities. Is that thing in your life truly giving you a sense of satisfaction? If you pursued it for all eternity, would you say that you were truly living? Haggai calls you to turn your attention to the foundation. There is no other Foundation for life than Jesus Christ. If you will receive Him and spend your life living for Him, then you will find that you are truly living.

CHAPTER 38

SEEN IN THE HUMBLE
ZECHARIAH

God could have announced the birth of Messiah with angels singing to the entire city of Jerusalem. Instead He told a few shepherds on a hill. Jesus could have been born in a King's palace. Instead He was born in a barn. Jesus could have been attended by the care of a thousand servants. Instead His hands grew rough using carpenter's tools. He could have been born to the most highly esteemed mother in Israel. Instead He chose a woman whose reputation was ruined by a pregnancy story that few believed.

Jesus could have chosen for Himself the most handsome body that Israel had ever seen. Instead He chose to have "no form or comeliness that anyone would desire Him" (Isaiah 53:2). When it came time to present Himself to Jerusalem as their King, He could have entered the city riding a brilliant white steed. Instead He came riding on a donkey. The choices that He made defy the expectations of man, but they demonstrate a key quality of the King of Kings—

humility. They also fulfill a number of prophecies, including important ones in the Book of Zechariah.

The Triumphal Entry into Jerusalem was a key event in the history of the world. Daniel wrote 500 years before it happened and foretold the exact date that it would occur, March 29th, 33 AD (Daniel 9:24-26). Like Daniel, Zechariah prophesied while the Jews were in exile. He also spoke of the Triumphal Entry, focusing on the humility of the King who would come on that day.

Rejoice greatly, O daughter of Zion! Shout in triumph, O daughter of Jerusalem! Behold, your king is coming to you; He is just and endowed with salvation, humble, and mounted on a donkey, even on a colt, the foal of a donkey (Zechariah 9:9).

When the day came, Jesus entered the city on a donkey. Also according to the prophecy, He was greeted by triumphant shouts. He came for the purpose of salvation, just not the kind that the crowds expected. The crowds wanted deliverance from Roman oppression but Jesus brought deliverance from the oppression of sin. The greatest problem that the people had was their own unrighteousness. They were unjust and rightly under the wrath of God. So they needed someone who was just and who could impute His righteousness to them. They needed the Humble King Jesus to die for their sins. If only for a day and if only for selfish reasons, they welcomed Him as He entered the city of Jerusalem.

The disciples went and did just as Jesus had instructed them, and brought the donkey and the colt, and laid their coats on them; and He sat on the coats. Most of the crowd spread their coats on the road, and others were cutting branches from the trees and spreading them in the road. The crowds going ahead of Him, and those who followed, were shouting, "Hosanna to the Son of David; Blessed is He who comes in the name of the Lord; Hosanna in the highest!" When He had entered Jerusalem, all the city was stirred, saying, "Who is this?" (Matthew 21:6-10).

The crowds recognized Jesus as a great prophet. Had they been able to discern the Old Testament Scriptures, they would have recognized that the prophet riding on the donkey was also the King of Kings and Lord of Lords. His humility in presenting Himself on a donkey is noteworthy, and so is His humility in allowing Himself to be betrayed and handed over for crucifixion. It was not as if Jesus didn't know what Judas had in his heart to do. "What you are going to do, do quickly" (John 13:27), Jesus said to Judas the night before Jesus died. What Judas was destined to do was also foretold by Zechariah.

I said to them, "If it is good in your sight, give me my wages; but if not, never mind!" So they weighed out thirty shekels of silver as my wages. Then the Lord said to me, "Throw it to the potter, that magnificent price at which I was valued by them." So I took the thirty shekels of silver and threw them to the potter in the house of the Lord (Zechariah 11:12-13).

The people did not value the prophetic ministry of Zechariah. But little did they know that their actions and his response were prophetic foreshadowing of an important event in the life of Messiah. Jesus was the Savior of the world, but Judas Iscariot valued Jesus' life so little that Judas betrayed Jesus into the hands of sinful men. Five specific details in the prophecy are so precise that they defy any attempt to chalk them up to coincidence.

First, the true prophet is rejected.

Second, a value is placed on his life and ministry. Judas accepts a bribe to betray Jesus. The price was 30 shekels of silver!

Third, that money actually gets thrown down at the feet of the ones who offered it. Judas, seized with guilt, cast the money at the religious leaders' feet.

Fourth, the place where the money is to be cast down is "the house of the Lord"—the temple in Jerusalem.

Fifth and finally, the religious leaders use Judas' money to buy a potter's field, calling it "Akeldama", meaning "Field of Blood". Truly it was purchased with blood money.

Jesus had the knowledge and power to avert His suffering, but He humbly accepted it in order to pay for the sins of others. "Being found in appearance as a man, He humbled Himself by becoming obedient to the point of death, even death on a cross" (Philippians 2:8). Jesus' three-fold humiliation (Divinity taking on human flesh, Innocence dying for the sins of others, Holiness subjected to the shame and torture of being lifted up naked on the beams of crucifixion) sets Him apart as the most humble man who ever lived.

Zechariah prophesied both Jesus' exuberant welcome while riding an untrained donkey and His underhanded betrayal into the hands of sinful men. They provide reason enough for us to believe in the Humble King—Jesus of Nazareth. He is the infinitely valuable Son of God, yet He is humble enough to allow Himself to be valued at 30 shekels of silver. He did this in order to fulfill the prophecies and to offer His life as a ransom for many.

CHAPTER 39

SEEN IN THE PROPHETS

Malachi

When Bible readers complete the few pages of the last Old Testament book, the Book of Matthew and the rest of the New Testament immediately greets them. But it must be stated that during the construction of the Bible, more than 400 years passed between the completion of the Old Testament and the start of the New Testament. This is vitally important because it removes any doubt that all of the prophecies of the 39 Old Testament books were penned long before Jesus appeared. The Hebrew Bible had already been translated into multiple languages by that time. There are even many extant fragments of the Hebrew Scriptures (the Dead Sea Scrolls) that scientists date to be prior to the time of Christ.

This inter-testamental period has come to be known as the "400 years of silence". By the time of Jesus, what was regarded as Scripture was set in stone. The Hebrews had no disagreement that each of the 39 books should be regarded as having come from God. Since Jesus fulfilled hundreds of prophecies within them proves that the Hebrews were right. The last of the books of the Old Testament—Malachi—tells of the coming of one more prophet who would serve as the forerunner who announces the appearance of Messiah.

Israel was always prone to wandering away from God. Elijah was a great prophet that God sent to draw them back from the brink of destruction. Most of Israel had bowed the knee to the false God Baal, so Elijah hosted a showdown between Baal and the one true God—Yahweh. God answered with fire, and the hearts of the people turned back to Him. Over the years, the people continued to wander, and God continued to send prophets to correct their course. The last Old Testament prophet—Malachi—would initiate 400 years of silence, and the people would need to wait for a prophet like Elijah to break the silence.

"Behold, I am going to send My messenger, and He will clear the way before Me. And the Lord, whom you seek, will suddenly come to His temple; and the messenger of the covenant, in whom you delight, behold, He is coming," says the Lord of Hosts (Malachi 3:1).

Jesus is described in five ways in this passage. He is the **Lord**, which means that He is actually God. He is **sought**, which means that He is the long-awaited hope of Israel. He suddenly **comes** to the Temple, which Jesus did at His Triumphal Entry (and turned the tables upside down!). He brings a New **Covenant**, which Jesus did with His own blood. He is the **delight** of all who look to Him for salvation.

But notice in the passage that there is one who goes ahead of

Jesus to "clear the way" for Him. As prophets do, this one will call Israel back to Yahweh. As prophesied, John the Baptist was sent as this final prophet, this special messenger who clears the way for the Lord Jesus Christ.

John the Baptist appeared in the wilderness preaching a baptism of repentance for the forgiveness of sins. And all the country of Judea was going out to him, and all the people of Jerusalem; and they were being baptized by him in the Jordan River, confessing their sins. John was clothed with camel's hair and wore a leather belt around his waist, and his diet was locusts and wild honey. And he was preaching, and saying, "After me One is coming who is mightier than I, and I am not fit to stoop down and untie the thong of His sandals. I baptized you with water; but He will baptize you with the Holy Spirit" (Mark 1:4-8).

The 39 books of Hebrew Scriptures amount to more than a thousand pages in many English translations. But the last two sentences do not leave the reader with a sense of closure. Quite the opposite, they leave the reader anticipating the fulfillment of a prophetic marker. Unless God sends the Messiah, there is no hope. Remember the Law of Moses and seek to keep it, but unless God initiates a New Covenant, no one will be found righteous. The Messiah alone can break the curse of sin. Those who believe in Him will welcome the day of His coming. The lost will think it is terrible. When the Father is well pleased to send Him, when the Father's predetermined time has arrived, the Messiah will come. Israel should know it when a prophet like Elijah appears on the scene. The Old Testament ends with this prophetic marker.

Behold, I am going to send you Elijah the prophet before the coming of the great and terrible day of the Lord. He will restore the hearts of the fathers to their children and the hearts of the children to their fathers, so that I will not come and smite the land with a curse (Malachi 4:5-6).

When John the Baptist appeared, the Israelites who were alive at the time should have recognized that it was time for Messiah to come and break the curse of sin and death. But even if most did not, you and I are called to recognize the signs that point to Him. John the Baptist was himself a great prophet. But like all the prophets who went before him, John the Baptist was only a forerunner of the Mighty One, the thongs of whose sandals none of us are worthy to untie. The prophecies of the 39 books all tie together in revealing Him. No one can break them or untie them, for they are all fulfilled in the person and work of Jesus Christ.

CONCLUSION

SEEING JESUS THROUGH THE EYES OF FAITH

Faith is precious. Those who have it—have real life that never ends. Those who don't—wish there was more to life. Faith has at least three characteristics.

First, it involves things not seen. It pertains to things that cannot be perceived by any of the five senses. That is to say, faith is a different kind of seeing.

Second, it rises beyond wishful thinking to the level of extreme confidence. There is an assurance—a sureness—in the heart of the one who has it. It is a deep-seated conviction.

Third, it rests upon a promise. It's not just any worldview that includes a supernatural element. It amounts to trusting a Person, because the one who has faith considers the words of the Object of his faith to be reliable. For this reason, faith is not blind. Faith is taking God at His Word.

It is a common error to say that God requires "a blind leap of faith". This expression conveys the idea that faith is baseless. This would be the case if God had never spoken. Had He not, faith would be entirely subjective. Whatever a person conceives would be as good an object of faith as any other. Each person could go with whatever they thought best. This would be blind faith, and it would be nothing more than individual human reasoning. But genuine faith is a response to something outside of oneself. So the Object of one's faith is what matters most. If there truly is a God, then trusting Him means trusting what He says.

Who do you say that Jesus is? Will you go so far as to say that He is a great prophet? Will you say that He is a great moral teacher? Will you look to Him as an example to follow? Is He someone with a special connection to divine realities? Is He tapped into the cosmos? Is He in touch with the Universe? Is He just a revolutionary Jewish Rabbi from the first century?

No matter what anyone else says of Him, God has provided 39 books of revelation to establish the matter definitively. He provided each of these books at least 400 years before sending Jesus to earth. In this way, each of us is responsible to recognize Him and take God at His Word. So it is not *blind faith* that God is after. He requires *faith in His Word.* Who is Jesus, not according to you or I, but according to the 39 books of Old Testament Scripture?

Jesus is the God, Man, King, Priest, Sacrifice, Yahweh, Savior, Passover Lamb, Blood Atonement, Raised Serpent, Prophet, Captain, Deliverer, Redeemer, Rejected King, Davidic King, King of Peace, Miracle Worker, Ark of Salvation, Slow Judge, Fast Friend, Strong Defender, Great Reversal, Forsaken, Crucified, Word, Meaning of

Life, Loving Husband, Virgin-born Son, Suffering Servant, New Covenant Maker, Weeping Prophet, Glory of the Lord, Messiah the Prince, Faithful Husband, Baptizer, Defender of the Weak, Betrayed by a Brother, Resurrected, Bethlehem Born, Wrath Satisfaction, Our Righteousness, Divider, Foundation, Humble, Prophesied Christ.

Entire books of Hebrew Scripture reveal that Jesus is each of these things. Within those books, specific details prove the overarching idea. Recall for example that Psalm 22 pictures a forsaken Son. But the specific details that precisely describe Christ's crucifixion must not be ignored. There are 22 of them, and each one ratchets up the conversation to the next level. He is not only surrounded by evil men, but they even gamble for His clothes. He not only suffers as His tongue cleaves to the roof of His mouth, but He is even pierced through His hands and feet.

Details pile up as evidence. Isaiah (52:13-53:12) chimes in and contributes the meaning of His death. Every one of the verses therein easily applies to Jesus dying for the purpose of taking the sin of the world upon Himself. From Abraham figuratively sacrificing Isaac to the blood of the Passover Lamb to Levitical sacrifices, everything points to this central idea that God has provided the blood of Jesus in order to atone for sin. There is simply too much evidence to push aside.

Would someone rather say that it was mere coincidence that Micah foretold where Messiah must be born and Jesus just so happened to be born there in Bethlehem? Should we make nothing of the fact that 173,880 days passed from Artaxerxes' command to rebuild Jerusalem until Jesus entered Jerusalem only to be cut off? Wasn't it strange in the first place that Daniel described two events and set a number to the duration between them? But when "69 sevens" yields 483 and this number is multiplied by the 360 days on the Hebrew Calendar and the result is 173,880 days, isn't this reason to at least raise an eyebrow?

If not the humble King, then who is this man who rides into Jerusalem on a donkey? Why does He come down from the Eastern Mountain, enter through the Eastern Gate, pass the threshold and enter in the Temple? What glory does He have that would embolden Him to overturn tables when He arrived?

Who was that strange prophet dunking people in the Jordan, eating locusts and honey? Why did he say that one Mightier than he was coming to baptize with the Holy Spirit and fire? Why did Judas throw those 30 pieces of silver on the Temple Floor? Why is this field called Akeldama? These are the kind of questions with which we are forced to wrestle if we refuse to believe that Jesus is who He is. Could it be that Jesus really is the Son of God?

What then did Jesus say about Himself? He claimed to be God! "Before Abraham was even born, I AM" (John 8:58). The student of the book of Exodus will recognize the memorial name of God and recognize Jesus' self-disclosure. At other times, Jesus claimed to be able to forgive sin. Who but God is able to do that? On multiple occasions, Jesus accepted worship, something that only God should receive. He did not deny that He was equal in being to God the Father. When pressed on this question, He only doubled down.

Overwhelming evidence has been set before you. Nevertheless, flesh and blood has not revealed the identity of Jesus Christ. After Jesus ascended into heaven, He poured out His Holy Spirit upon the believers. He continues to do so today. He placed the fire in my soul that made me passionate to write this book. All I did was present what is clearly written in the Old Testament. But my heart burned with passion every day that I wrote. The Holy Spirit was pleased to use an unworthy vessel like me to bring you the message about Jesus. He is also the only One who can convince you about the truth of it. It is my prayer, and I believe that God will answer it, that as you think about the words of the Scripture, your heart will be strangely warmed. My prayer for you, friend, is that the Holy Spirit will draw you to faith in Jesus Christ.

Jesus is the Son of God. He died on the cross, was buried, and rose from the dead. This He did in order to save you from your sins. He truly loves you. As the greatest friend, He laid down His life in your place. He took the death penalty that you and I deserve. Having risen from the dead, Jesus has opened the way for you and I to have eternal life. God will gladly forgive your sins if you place your trust in His Son. Believe in the Lord Jesus Christ and you will be saved.

If you find yourself believing as you read these words, then why not pray right now and invite Jesus Christ to take away your sins and become your Lord and Savior? Tell Him that you repent of your sins. Ask for forgiveness. Ask for deliverance, so that you are not controlled by sin anymore. Just call upon Jesus to save you.

If you did that, then please find a Bible-believing Church in your area to attend. I am part of an Evangelical Free Church of America congregation, and there is probably one near where you live too. But there are many wonderful churches across America and all around the world. The key is finding a faithful church that has not forsaken the Word of God or denied Christ's Name.

Once you have a true church, you should be baptized. This is a symbolic act, but it is also important. By going under the water and coming up, you identify with Christ's death and resurrection. It is the first step of obedience that you need to take, which will demonstrate that you have new life in Him.

It is also important that you get a Bible and begin reading. Even a little bit each day can make all the difference in your new life, now that you are a Christian (which you are if you genuinely believe in Jesus). Finally, pray all the time. You can do so in the privacy of your own mind or out loud among other believers, but talk to your God and Savior.

If you have not yet placed your faith in Jesus, I pray that you will, and I implore you to do so very soon. We do not know when the Day of the Lord will arrive. We do not know the day of our own death. That is why it is so important to receive the words of Hebrews 4:7, which are also quoted from the Old Testament (Psalm 95), "Today if you hear his voice, do not harden you hearts".

ABOUT THE AUTHOR

Jeff Kliewer resides in New Jersey with his wife and two children. He graduated from Dallas Theological Seminary with a Masters Degree in Cross-Cultural Ministry. From 2004 to 2016, he worked as a missionary to Philadelphia. In 2016, he became Senior Pastor of Cornerstone Church in Mt. Laurel, New Jersey. Jeff's life ambition is to know Christ and to make Him known.

Made in the USA
Coppell, TX
12 May 2020

25210195R00139